30 DAY PULSES CHALLENGE

30 Day Pulses Challenge

Pulse Cookbook with 30 Day Superfood Meal Plan

By: Carly Rae

30 DAY PULSES CHALLENGE

30 DAY PULSES CHALLENGE

Legal notice

This book is copyright (c) 2017 by Carly Rae. All rights are reserved. This book may not be duplicated or copied, either in whole or in part, via any means including any electronic form of duplication such as recording or transcription. The contents of this book may not be transmitted, stored in any retrieval system, or copied in any other manner regardless of whether use is public or private without express prior permission of the publisher.

This book provides information only. The author does not offer any specific advice, including medical advice, nor does the author suggest the reader or any other person engage in any particular course of conduct in any specific situation. This book is not intended to be used as a substitute for any professional advice, medical or of any other variety. The reader accepts sole responsibility for how he or she uses the information contained in this book. Under no circumstances will the publisher or the author be held liable for damages of any kind arising either directly or indirectly from any information contained in this book.

30 DAY PULSES CHALLENGE

30 DAY PULSES CHALLENGE

Table of Contents

Introduction 10
   Pulses: An Essential Part of a Healthy Life 12
   Pulses: Weight Loss Helpers 14
   Pulses: What Kinds Are There? 16
Pulses: How to Buy, Store and Prepare Your Pulses 17
Day 1 19
Green Peas Creamy Salads 19
Baked Chickpeas Falafel 21
Chickpeas Classic Loaf 23
Day 2 26
Sweet Beans in Egg Blanket 26
Lentils Salads with Lemon Dressing 28
Hot and Spicy Green Peas with Beef 30
Day 3 32
Scrambled Lentils Veggie 32
Green Peas Salads with Fried Mushroom 35
Creamy Lentils Soup 36
Day 4 39
Nutritious Green Breakfast 39
Beans and Lentils Tacos 41
Mixed Lentils Rice 43
Day 5 45
Beans on Toast 45
Simple Steamed Fava Beans 47
Sweet Sour Lentils with Chorizo 49
Day 6 51
Nutritious Mung Beans Milk 51
Green Peas Pasta 53
Kidney Beans and Beef Soup 55
Day 7 57
Green Peas Cabbage Salads 57
Savory Lentils in Coconut Cream 59

5

30 DAY PULSES CHALLENGE

White Beans in Red 61
Day 8 63
Green Peas Omelets 63
Chickpeas Tomato Salads 65
Lentils Slices with Sweet Potato 67
Day 9 69
Nutritious Green Peas Salads 69
Beans Burrito with Peanut Sauce 71
Lentils Turmeric Soup 73
Day 10 75
Nutritious Mashed Lentils 75
Delicious Beans Fritter 77
Sautéed Kidney Beans with Carrots 79
Day 11 81
White Beans Crumbles with Peas and Cheese ... 81
Natural Sweet Beans Salads 83
Chickpeas Curry with Cabbage 85
Day 12 88
Nutritious Chickpeas, Green Peas, and Beef 88
Green Peas Samosa 90
Baked Lentils with Cheese 92
Day 13 94
Green Feta Salads 94
Tasty Lentils Burger 96
Original Mixed Beans Stew 98
Day 14 100
Healthy Cannellini Beans with Spinach 100
Spicy Lentils and Peas Balls 102
Inspired Lentils with Pork and Quinoa 103
Day 15 104
Chickpeas Egg Porridge 105
Black-eyed Peas Salads with Zucchini 108
Kidney Beans Garlic 110
Day 16 111
Lentils Porridge with Orange Sauce 111

30 DAY PULSES CHALLENGE

Delicious Beans Pie 114
Cannellini Mushroom Soup.................................... 116
Day 17... 117
Mung Beans Porridge with Coconut Milk.......... 117
Cheesy Black Beans in Wrap.................................. 120
Lentils Stew with Green Peas................................ 122
Day 18... 124
Sweet Soy Lentils Sushi 124
Chickpeas and Fava Beans Fried Balls............... 127
Healthy Beans Soup with Veggie......................... 129
Day 19... 131
Kidney Beans Thick Soup 131
Lentils Coconut Burger 133
Garbanzo Beans with Green Kale........................ 135
Day 20... 137
Spiced Green Peas.. 137
Lentils Pasta with Goat Cheese............................. 139
Delicious Fava Beans with Browned Chicken. 140
Day 21... 143
Green Peas Casserole... 143
Scrumptious Indian red Lentils............................ 145
Baked Beans with Pork.. 147
Day 22... 149
Soft Waffle with Green Peas.................................. 149
White Beans Tomato Macaroni 151
Warm Lentils Soup with Spinach........................ 153
Day 23... 155
Soft Beans Patties.. 155
Spicy Lentils Noodles 157
Red Hot Green Peas... 159
Day 24... 161
Scrambled Lentils Veggie....................................... 161
Beans and Shrimps in Tomato Pond 163
Green Peas in Mixed Vegetables 164
Day 25... 166

30 DAY PULSES CHALLENGE

Creamy Mung Beans Milk Porridge 166
Delicious Lentils Salmon 168
Hot Beans Rice 170
Day 26 172
Chickpeas Honey Salads 172
Cheesy Bean Lasagna 174
Spicy Black Beans Turkey 176
Day 27 178
Healthy Colorful Salads 178
Mixed Beans and Peas Salads 180
Smooth Green Peas Soup 181
Day 28 183
Nourishing Beans and Shrimps 183
Chickpeas Bites with Curry Spices 185
Kidney Beans Stew 187
Day 29 189
Cheesy Lentils Tender 189
Savory Lentils Rolls 191
Chickpeas in Tomato Gravy 193
Day 30 195
Green Peas Pancake 195
Beans Avocado Salads 197
Lentils Balls Tomato Soup 198

8

30 DAY PULSES CHALLENGE

Introduction

Health problems like strokes, type 2 diabetes, cancer, heart attack, hypertension, high cholesterol, obesity, and other chronic diseases are becoming more and more common. The number of people that suffer from these problems is increasing all the time. These diseases do not discriminate on the basis of age as old and young alike are suffering from these problems.

People may not always realize it, but these diseases are the scariest thing out there. They can destroy lives in such a short amount of time. They steal life just like a thief can steal from us. They take from us when we are unprepared and destroy the normal life that we once held dear. Because these diseases are able to destroy lives and in many cases cures do not exist or are uncertain, we need focus on prevention.

There are two questions that we need to pose: how do we work towards this solution, and how can we eradicate these diseases from our everyday lives?

Most health problems can be related back to the individuals eating habits. Today, people are eating worse than ever. We're busy all day long and choose instant options without really considering what the consequences will be for our bodies. All that junk food and fast food may be easy for people that are constantly on the move, but it can really wreak havoc with your body.

Fast food and heavily processed frozen foods seem to fit nicely into our busy lifestyles, but they are the worst choice. They don't have much nutrition if they have any at all and they are often full of excess fats and sugar. The lack of nutrition and the high-fat content of these fast foods are part of what causes the chronic diseases that we mentioned before.

In order to prevent these diseases, you will have to pay more attention to the food that you are eating. You will have to start avoiding junk foods and replacing those with more nutrient rich and healthy foods. This is the first step to living healthier. So, you will need to start looking at whether or not the food is good for you before you put it in your mouth.

While you may assume that good food is found in expensive meals, but that isn't true. Good foods are the ones that have a lot of vitamins, minerals, fiber, complex nutrient-rich carbs, and healthy fats. One of the best foods for this kind of nutrition is known as pulses.

30 DAY PULSES CHALLENGE

Pulses: An Essential Part of a Healthy Life

Pulses are eaten all around the world as staples in a healthy diet. You'll find them especially in countries like Pakistan and India. Pulses are acknowledged as healthy food by plenty of other civilizations too. Internationally, pulses are not recognized for the value that they truly have. This is because pulses are often regarded as food that only poor people eat. Instead of eating meat, many people will use pulses as a source of protein when money is tight. In the west, pulses are generally seen as a cheap and inferior alternative to meat, however this is simply not true.

Even though we underestimate pulses, their benefit is quite amazing. Pulses like peas, lentils, beans, and chickpeas are low fat, low sodium, rich in iron, rich in protein, and full of all the vitamins and nutrients that are necessary for our bodies.

Pulses are a great source of protein. When compared to grains like corn, rice, and wheat, pulses have twice the protein content. This protein content can improve your immune system as well as keep your body strong.

Pulses contain plenty of good carbohydrates. Good carbohydrates like starches and fiber allow the body to feel full for longer periods of time. They can also help your body digest other foods that you are eating.

Pulses have plenty of minerals and vitamins. While this fact alone may make you want to eat more pulses, you should also consider the fact that pulses have low fat and sugar content.

30 DAY PULSES CHALLENGE

When you eat pulses, you lower your risk of developing diabetes as there will be less sugar in your diet. Pulses also help to reduce cholesterol and will help you control your blood pressure. Blood pressure and cholesterol can influence how susceptible you are to heart diseases.
Pulses are full of great nutrients for your body. These nutrients will allow your body to work so much better and make sure that your metabolism is up to speed. This will definitely improve your life.

30 DAY PULSES CHALLENGE

Pulses: Weight Loss Helpers

Reaching that ideal weight is something that many people strive for. Many people that don't think that their body is perfect yet will work their hardest to try and reach that weight that they believe will improve their appearance. Diets are one of the methods that people use to try and reach those weight goals.

Well, appearances may be a little bit of a superficial goal, however it is true that reaching a healthy weight will have many benefits to your overall well-being. A healthy body will have a better immune system, more energy throughout the day, and be able to avoid diseases that could easily tear apart your life.

With these goals in mind, people have to find the most effective path to that healthy weight. A diet should be chosen to make sure that you are getting the right kind of nutrients as well as help you lose excess weight. It shouldn't just be one or the other. Pulses are a great ingredient to include in your diet because of how much nutrition you can get from them and how full they will keep you feeling which makes losing weight almost effortless.

As explained above, pulses contain a lot of protein, fiber, and other healthy carbohydrates. However, the healthy parts of the pulses aren't just about the nutrients involved. Pulses will help stimulate your gastric hormones. This will help you feel full for longer periods of times. This will help you eat less during the day. This is also because of the amount of fiber that is found in pulses.

30 DAY PULSES CHALLENGE

If you're eating pulses consistently, then you'll find that you'll be losing weight on a regular basis. Even when you reach your weight goal, you shouldn't stop eating pulses. They will allow you to maintain your weight.

30 DAY PULSES CHALLENGE

Pulses: What Kinds Are There?
If you want to add more pulses to your diet, you'll need to know what to look for. Refer to this list next time you are at the grocery store.

Peas
Whole or split yellow peas
Whole or split green peas
Lentils
Large green lentils
Regular green lentils
Red lentils
Split red lentils
Beans
Navy beans
White beans
Black beans
Kidney beans
Pinto beans
Cannellini beans
Black-eyed peas
Chickpeas
Garbanzo chickpeas
Kala chana chickpeas

Pulses: How to Buy, Store and Prepare Your Pulses

After getting some information about pulses and how they can improve your health, you're ready to get started with adding them to your diet. Here are some tips on how to best purchase, store, and prepare pulses.

When purchasing pulses, you will want to pick ones that have bright colors, have a uniform size, and are smooth. If you buy dry pulses, then you will want to store them in a jar with a tight seal. Glass jars are the best kind of jars to use. Once you have put them in a jar, you will want to keep them in a cool, dark, and dry place.

You can use canned pulses without too much worry. You will need to remember to drain and rinse the pulses before using them to reduce the amount of sodium you are putting into your recipes.

Lentils and split peas don't require soaking before you add them to your recipes. Other pulses like beans, chickpeas, and whole peas will need to be soaked before you use them in a recipe.

After soaking pulses, you will need to rinse and lightly wash them. This gets rids of extra sugars and carbohydrates, as well as toxins that occur naturally in some dried pulses like beans.

Instead of preparing small batches of pulses, you can save time by soaking and cooking pulses in larger batches. After the whole batch is done, then you can divide up the pulses into about one cup portions for storage. In the fridge, they will last for a week. In the freezer, they will last for six months.

30 DAY PULSES CHALLENGE

Pulses	Soaking Time	Cooking Time
Split lentils	No need to soak	20 minutes
Split peas	At least 2 hours	30 minutes
Whole lentils	At least 2 hours	30 minutes
Mung beans	At least 2 hours	40 minutes
Black-eyed beans	Overnight	60 minutes
Kidney beans	Overnight	75 minutes
Cannellini beans	Overnight	75 minutes
Pinto beans	Overnight	75 minutes
Black beans	Overnight	75 minutes
Chickpeas	Overnight	75 minutes

30 DAY PULSES CHALLENGE

Day 1

Breakfast : Green Peas Creamy Salads
Lunch : Baked Chickpeas Falafel
Dinner : Chickpeas Classic Loaf

Green Peas Creamy Salads

Serving: 2

Nutrition Facts
Servings: 2
Per Serving
Calories 203
Total Fat 8.6g
Saturated Fat 5.2g
Trans Fat 0g
Cholesterol 25mg
Sodium 121mg
Potassium 347mg
Total Carb 23.8g
Dietary Fiber 4.6g
Sugars 11.2g
Protein 8.7g
Nutrition Facts
Servings: 2
Per Serving
Calories 203

Ingredients:

1 cup frozen green peas

½ cup diced carrots

1-tablespoon butter

30 DAY PULSES CHALLENGE

1 tablespoon chopped onion

¼ teaspoon pepper

1-tablespoon multi purpose flour

1-cup milk

Directions:

- Pour water in a pot then bring to boil.
- Once it is boiled, place the green peas in the pot then cooks for 2 minutes until tender. Set aside.
- Combine milk with flour then stir until incorporated.
- Melt the butter on a saucepan over medium heat.
- Once the butter is melted, stir in chopped onion then sautés until wilted and aromatic.
- Next, add peas and carrot into the saucepan then pour the milk mixture into the saucepan.
- Season with pepper then brings to a simmer.
- Transfer to a serving dish then enjoy immediately.

30 DAY PULSES CHALLENGE

Baked Chickpeas Falafel

Serving: 4

Nutrition Facts
Servings: 4
Per Serving
Calories 157
Total Fat 8.6g
Saturated Fat 1.2g
Trans Fat 0g
Cholesterol 0mg
Sodium 9mg
Potassium 260mg
Total Carb 16.4g
Dietary Fiber 4.7g
Sugars 2.9g
Protein 5.1g
Nutrition Facts
Servings: 4
Per Serving
Calories 157

Ingredients:

2 tablespoons olive oil

½ cup cooked chickpeas

2 tablespoons chopped onion

4 tablespoons chopped parsley

4 tablespoons cilantro

1 teaspoon minced garlic

¼ teaspoon cumin

¼ teaspoon cinnamon

¼ teaspoon black pepper

30 DAY PULSES CHALLENGE

Directions:

- Preheat an oven to 375 F then coat a baking sheet with olive oil. Set aside.
- Place the cooked chickpeas in a food processor together with chopped onion, chopped parsley, olive oil, cilantro, minced garlic, cinnamon, cumin, and black pepper. Process until incorporated and smooth.
- Shape the mixture into small patties form then arrange on the prepared baking sheet.
- Bake for about 13 minutes then flip them and continue to bake for another 13 minutes or until both side of the falafels are brown.
- Once it is done, transfer to a serving dish. Enjoy!

30 DAY PULSES CHALLENGE

Chickpeas Classic Loaf

Serving: 12

Nutrition Facts
Servings: 12
Per Serving
Calories 273
Total Fat 7.6g
Saturated Fat 1.1g
Trans Fat 0g
Cholesterol 0mg
Sodium 167mg
Potassium 542mg
Total Carb 40.7g
Dietary Fiber 9.9g
Sugars 7.9g
Protein 12.1g
Nutrition Facts
Servings: 12
Per Serving
Calories 273

Ingredients:

3 cups cooked chickpeas

¼ cup chopped onion

2 tablespoons chopped celery

¼ cup grated carrots

2 teaspoons minced garlic

1-½ cup breadcrumbs

½ cup soymilk

2 tablespoons Worcestershire sauce

1-tablespoon soy sauce

2 tablespoons olive oil

2 tablespoons flax seeds

2 tablespoons tomato paste

1-teaspoon liquid smoke

¼ teaspoon black pepper

SAUCE:

¼ cup chopped cashew

¼ cup water

2 teaspoons tamarind

1 teaspoons brown sugar

1 teaspoon minced garlic

1 ½ teaspoons soy sauce

Directions:

- Preheat an oven to 375 F then coats a medium loaf pan with cooking oil. Set aside.
- Place chickpeas in a food processor together with onion, celery, carrots, breadcrumbs, olive oil, and soymilk.
- Season with garlic, Worcestershire sauce, flax seeds, tomato paste, liquid smoke, and black pepper. Using your hand, mix until combined.
- Transfer the mixture to the prepared loaf pan then spread evenly.
- Bake for 30 minutes until the top is lightly brown.
- Meanwhile, combine all of the sauce ingredients in a saucepan.

30 DAY PULSES CHALLENGE

- Cook over low heat while stirring occasionally until thickened.
- When the chickpeas loaf is completely cooked, remove from the oven then place on a serving dish.
- Drizzle the sauce over the loaf then serve immediately.

30 DAY PULSES CHALLENGE

Day 2

Breakfast : Sweet Beans in Egg Blanket
Lunch : Lentils Salads with Lemon Dressing
Dinner : Hot and Spicy Green Peas

Sweet Beans in Egg Blanket

Serving: 4

Nutrition Facts
Servings: 4
Per Serving
Calories 230
Total Fat 7.9g
Saturated Fat 1.9g
Trans Fat 0g
Cholesterol 164mg
Sodium 76mg
Potassium 593mg
Total Carb 29.8g
Dietary Fiber 5.8g
Sugars 3.6g
Protein 13.3g
Nutrition Facts
Servings: 4
Per Serving
Calories 230

Ingredients:

2 teaspoons olive oil

½ cup cooked kidney beans

2 tablespoons corn kernels

30 DAY PULSES CHALLENGE

¼ cup chopped onion

½ teaspoon pepper

4 organic eggs

Vegetable oil, to fry

Directions:

- Preheat a skillet over medium heat then pour olive oil into it.
- Once it is hot, stir in chopped onion then sautés until wilted and aromatic.
- Add the kidney beans and corn kernels into the skillet then season with pepper.
- Stirring occasionally and cook until the kidney beans and corn kernels are completely seasoned and tender. Set aside.
- Crack the eggs then place in a bowl.
- Using a whisker whisk the eggs until completely beaten then makes 4 thin omelets.
- Place the omelets on a flat surface then drop about 2 tablespoons of the filling on each omelet.
- Tightly roll the sheets until becoming logs.
- Arrange on a serving dish then enjoy immediately.

30 DAY PULSES CHALLENGE

Lentils Salads with Lemon Dressing

Serving: 4

Nutrition Facts
Servings: 4
Per Serving
Calories 236
Total Fat 7.6g
Saturated Fat 1.1g
Trans Fat 0g
Cholesterol 0mg
Sodium 12mg
Potassium 475mg
Total Carb 30.2g
Dietary Fiber 14.7g
Sugars 1.9g
Protein 12.6g
Nutrition Facts
Servings: 4
Per Serving
Calories 236

Ingredients:

1 cup green lentils

1 teaspoon minced garlic

3 teaspoons olive oil

2 tablespoons chopped celery

2 cups water

DRESSING:

2 tablespoons lemon juice

3 teaspoons olive oil

½ teaspoon Dijon mustard

½ teaspoon raw honey

½ teaspoon minced garlic

¼ teaspoon black pepper

Directions:

- Wash and rinse the lentils then places in a pot.
- Add 1 teaspoon of minced garlic and 3 teaspoons olive oil then pours water into the pot.
- Bring to boil and once it is boiled, reduce the heat then continue cooking until the lentils are tender.
- Meanwhile, prepare the dressing.
- Place all of the dressing ingredients then mix until combined.
- Transfer the cooked lentils to a serving dish then drizzle the dressing over the lentils. Mix well.
- Garnish with tomatoes and celery then enjoy!

30 DAY PULSES CHALLENGE

Hot and Spicy Green Peas with Beef

Serving: 4

Nutrition Facts
Servings: 2
Per Serving
Calories 245
Total Fat 7.9g
Saturated Fat 2.4g
Trans Fat 0g
Cholesterol 76mg
Sodium 269mg
Potassium 531mg
Total Carb 12.1g
Dietary Fiber 3.8g
Sugars 4.7g
Protein 30g
Nutrition Facts
Servings: 2
Per Serving
Calories 245

Ingredients:

1 cup frozen green peas

2 tablespoons chopped green chili

1-teaspoon olive oil

1 teaspoon minced garlic

1-teaspoon soy sauce

2 tablespoons ground beef

Directions:

- Pour water in a pot then bring to boil.

30 DAY PULSES CHALLENGE

- Once it is boiled, place the green peas in the pot then cooks for 2 minutes until tender. Set aside.
- Preheat a skillet over medium heat then pour olive oil into it.
- Once it is hot, stir in minced garlic then sauté until aromatic and lightly brown.
- Next, add ground beef into the skillet then stir until the beef is no longer pink.
- After that, toss the steamed green peas then drizzles soy sauce on top.
- Stir occasionally until all of the ingredients are completely cooked.
- Transfer to a serving dish then enjoy with a bowl of rice.

30 DAY PULSES CHALLENGE

Day 3

Breakfast : Scrambled Lentils Veggie
Lunch : Green Beans Casserole
Dinner : Creamy Lentils Soup

Scrambled Lentils Veggie

Serving: 4

Nutrition Facts
Servings: 4
Per Serving
Calories 229
Total Fat 5.1g
Saturated Fat 1.1g
Trans Fat 0g
Cholesterol 82mg
Sodium 35mg
Potassium 513mg
Total Carb 30.8g
Dietary Fiber 14.9g
Sugars 1.7g
Protein 15.4g
Nutrition Facts
Servings: 4
Per Serving
Calories 229

Ingredients:

1 cup uncooked lentils

2 organic eggs

2 teaspoons olive oil

1 teaspoon minced garlic

¼ cup chopped onion

¼ teaspoon pepper

¼ cup chopped leek

Directions:

- Place red lentils and yellow lentils in a pot then pour water over the lentils. Bring to boil.
- Once it is boil, covers the pot with the lid then reduces the heat.
- Cook for about 30 minutes until the lentils are tender.
- Strain the lentils then sets aside.
- Preheat a skillet over medium heat then pour olive oil into it.
- Once it is hot, stir in chopped onion and minced garlic then sauté until wilted and aromatic.
- Add the lentils into the skillet then dust pepper on top. Sauté until the lentils are completely seasoned.
- Crack the eggs then place in a bowl. Using a whisker, whisk the eggs until beaten.
- Pour the beaten eggs over the lentils then quickly stirs until becoming scrambled.
- After that, add chopped leek into the skillet then stir well.
- Transfer the scrambled lentils to a serving dish.

30 DAY PULSES CHALLENGE

- Serve and enjoy.

30 DAY PULSES CHALLENGE

Green Peas Salads with Fried Mushroom

Serving: 3

Nutrition Facts
Servings: 3
Per Serving
Calories 228
Total Fat 5g
Saturated Fat 1.2g
Trans Fat 0g
Cholesterol 1mg
Sodium 45mg
Potassium 139mg
Total Carb 31.3g
Dietary Fiber 5.5g
Sugars 2.1g
Protein 13.1g
Nutrition Facts
Servings: 3
Per Serving
Calories 228

Ingredients:

    1-cup cooked green peas

    1 tablespoon lemon juice

    ½ cup plain yogurt

    ¼ lb. oyster mushroom

    2 tablespoons rice flour

    1 teaspoon minced garlic

    2 tablespoons water

    Vegetable oil

30 DAY PULSES CHALLENGE

Directions:

- Combine rice flour with minced garlic and water then mix until incorporated.
- Preheat a non-stick pan over medium heat then pour vegetable oil into the pan.
- Dip the oyster mushroom in the rice flour mixture then put in the hot vegetable oil.
- Fry until lightly brown then drain the oil. Set aside.
- Combine cooked green peas with plain yogurt and lemon juice in a bowl. Mix until incorporated.
- Sprinkle fried mushroom on top then serve immediately.

Creamy Lentils Soup

Serving: 4

Nutrition Facts
Servings: 4
Per Serving
Calories 234
Total Fat 3.4g
Saturated Fat 0.5g
Trans Fat 0.1g
Cholesterol 0mg
Sodium 264mg
Potassium 598mg
Total Carb 37.5g
Dietary Fiber 15.6g
Sugars 3.9g
Protein 14g
Nutrition Facts
Servings: 4
Per Serving
Calories 234

Ingredients:

- 1 cup uncooked lentils
- 1 ½ teaspoons olive oil
- ½ cup chopped onion
- 1 teaspoon minced garlic
- 2 tablespoons chopped parsley
- ¼ teaspoon cumin
- ¼ cup mashed potato
- ¼ cup grated carrot
- 2 cups low sodium vegetable broth
- ¼ teaspoon pepper
- ½ cup soymilk

Directions:

- Preheat olive oil in a pot over medium heat.
- Stir in chopped onion and minced garlic then sauté until wilted and aromatic.
- Add chopped parsley and cumin into the pot then cook for about 2 minutes.
- Next, stir in lentils together with mashed potato and grated carrot then pour vegetable broth into the pot. Bring to boil.
- Once it is boil, season with pepper then cover the pot with the lid. Reduce the heat.
- Cook for about 30 minutes until the lentils are tender.
- After that, open the lid then pour soymilk over the soup. Bring to a simmer.

30 DAY PULSES CHALLENGE

- Once it is done, remove from the heat and let it warm.
- Using an immersion blender, blend the soup until smooth.
- Transfer to a soup bowl and enjoy warm.

30 DAY PULSES CHALLENGE

Day 4

Breakfast : Nutritious Green Breakfast
Lunch : Beans and Lentils Tacos
Dinner : Mixed Lentils Rice

Nutritious Green Breakfast

Serving: 8

Nutrition Facts
Servings: 8
Per Serving
Calories 211
Total Fat 8.1g
Saturated Fat 1.1g
Trans Fat 0g
Cholesterol 0mg
Sodium 9mg
Potassium 425mg
Total Carb 26.6g
Dietary Fiber 9.2g
Sugars 3.9g
Protein 9.8g
Nutrition Facts
Servings: 8
Per Serving
Calories 211

Ingredients:

¼ cup olive oil

1 cup cooked green peas

¼ cup chopped onion

30 DAY PULSES CHALLENGE

1 teaspoon minced garlic

¼ teaspoon black pepper

Directions:

- Pour water in a pot then bring to boil.
- Once it is boiled, place the green peas in the pot then cooks for 2 minutes until tender.

- Place the green peas in a food processor together with chopped onion, minced garlic, and black pepper. Process until incorporated and smooth.
- Shape the mixture into small balls form then chill in the refrigerator for 10 minutes.
- Preheat a non-stick pan over medium heat then pour olive oil into it.
- Take the balls out from the refrigerator then place in the pan.
- Fry for about 3 minutes until brown then flips and cook for another 3 minutes until all sides of the balls are brown.
- Once it is done, transfer to a serving dish. Enjoy!

30 DAY PULSES CHALLENGE

Beans and Lentils Tacos

Serving: 4

Nutrition Facts
Servings: 4
Per Serving
Calories 238
Total Fat 3.5g
Saturated Fat 0.5g
Trans Fat 0g
Cholesterol 0mg
Sodium 15mg
Potassium 600mg
Total Carb 40.1g
Dietary Fiber 12.6g
Sugars 1.5g
Protein 12.9g
Nutrition Facts
Servings: 4
Per Serving
Calories 238

Ingredients:

2 teaspoons olive oil

½ cup cooked kidney beans

½ cup uncooked lentils

¼ cup chopped onion

½ teaspoon pepper

4 tortillas

Directions:

- Place red lentils and yellow lentils in a pot then pour water over the lentils. Bring to boil.

30 DAY PULSES CHALLENGE

- Once it is boil, covers the pot with the lid then reduces the heat.
- Cook for about 30 minutes until the lentils are tender.
- Strain the lentils then sets aside.
- Preheat a skillet over medium heat then pour olive oil into it.
- Once it is hot, stir in chopped onion then sautés until wilted and aromatic.
- Add the cooked beans and lentils then season with pepper.
- Stirring occasionally and cook until the beans and carrot are completely seasoned and tender.
- Place the tortillas on a flat surface then drop about 2 tablespoons of cooked beans and lentils.
- Fold the tortillas into halves then place on a saucepan over medium heat.
- Brush the tortillas with oil then bake for about 2 minutes.
- Transfer to a serving dish then enjoy!

30 DAY PULSES CHALLENGE

Mixed Lentils Rice

Serving: 5

Nutrition Facts
Servings: 5
Per Serving
Calories 225
Total Fat 5g
Saturated Fat 0.5g
Trans Fat 0g
Cholesterol 0mg
Sodium 201mg
Potassium 389mg
Total Carb 32.8g
Dietary Fiber 12.7g
Sugars 1.3g
Protein 13.1g
Nutrition Facts
Servings: 5
Per Serving
Calories 225

Ingredients:

- 1 cup uncooked red lentils
- 1 cup uncooked yellow lentils
- 1-tablespoon olive oil
- ½ cup chopped onion
- 1-teaspoon pepper

Directions:

- Place red lentils and yellow lentils in a pot then pour water over the lentils. Bring to boil.

30 DAY PULSES CHALLENGE

- Once it is boil, covers the pot with the lid then reduces the heat.
- Cook for about 30 minutes until the lentils are tender.
- Strain the lentils then sets aside.
- Preheat a skillet over medium heat then pour olive oil into it.
- Once it is hot, stir in chopped onion then sautés until wilted and aromatic.
- Add the lentils into the skillet then dust pepper on top. Sauté until the lentils are completely seasoned.
- Transfer to a serving dish and enjoy warm.

30 DAY PULSES CHALLENGE

Day 5

Breakfast : Beans on Toast
Lunch : Simple Steamed Fava Beans
Dinner : Sweet Sour Lentils with Chorizo

Beans on Toast

Serving: 4

Nutrition Facts
Servings: 4
Per Serving
Calories 216
Total Fat 3.9g
Saturated Fat 1g
Trans Fat 0.2g
Cholesterol 82mg
Sodium 136mg
Potassium 765mg
Total Carb 31.9g
Dietary Fiber 7.3g
Sugars 2.2g
Protein 14.4g
Nutrition Facts
Servings: 4
Per Serving
Calories 216

Ingredients:

¾ cup cooked white beans

½ teaspoon pepper

¼ teaspoon nutmeg

30 DAY PULSES CHALLENGE

½ teaspoon olive oil

2 organic eggs

3 slices whole-wheat bread of your choice

Directions:

- Preheat a skillet over medium heat then pour olive oil into it.
- Stir in the beans together with the liquid. Season with pepper and nutmeg then bring to boil.
- Once it is boiled, reduce the heat and cook for about 15 minutes.
- When it is done, transfer to a dish then set aside.
- Preheat another pan and once it is hot, stir in the eggs. Quickly make scrambled egg then set aside as well.
- Place the whole-wheat on a flat surface then pour the beaten eggs.
- Top with cooked beans then arrange on a serving platter.
- Serve and enjoy!

30 DAY PULSES CHALLENGE

Simple Steamed Fava Beans

Serving: 4

Nutrition Facts
Servings: 4
Per Serving
Calories 258
Total Fat 1.2g
Saturated Fat 0.3g
Trans Fat 0g
Cholesterol 0mg
Sodium 22mg
Potassium 810mg
Total Carb 43.9g
Dietary Fiber 18.8g
Sugars 4.4g
Protein 19.7g
Nutrition Facts
Servings: 4
Per Serving
Calories 258

Ingredients:

 2 cups fava beans

 6 cups water

 2 tablespoons lemon juice

Directions:

- Pour water in a pot then brings to boil.
- Meanwhile, take the bean pods then remove the seams.
- After that, open the pods then take the beans out.
- Place the beans in the hot water and let them sit for about 30 seconds.

- Strain the cooked fava beans then transfer to a bowl with cold water. This process will help you to automatically remove the coat of the beans.
- Transfer the beans to a bowl then splash lemon juice on top. Toss to combine.
- Serve and enjoy immediately.

30 DAY PULSES CHALLENGE

Sweet Sour Lentils with Chorizo

Serving: 4

Nutrition Facts
Servings: 4
Per Serving
Calories 205
Total Fat 4.7g
Saturated Fat 0.8g
Trans Fat 0g
Cholesterol 2mg
Sodium 124mg
Potassium 365mg
Total Carb 32.2g
Dietary Fiber 11.3g
Sugars 9.7g
Protein 9.9g
Nutrition Facts
Servings: 4
Per Serving
Calories 205

Ingredients:

¾ cup uncooked lentils

¼ cup sliced chorizo

3 teaspoons olive oil

1 teaspoon chopped onion

1 bay leaf

1 tablespoon lemon juice

2 tablespoon mashed tomato

¼ teaspoon pepper

2 tablespoons raw honey

1-cup low sodium vegetable broth

30 DAY PULSES CHALLENGE

Directions:

- Place lentils in a pot then pour water over the lentils. Bring to boil.
- Once it is boil, covers the pot with the lid then reduces the heat.
- Cook for about 30 minutes until the lentils are tender.
- Strain the cooked lentils then set aside.
- Preheat a skillet over medium heat then pour olive oil into it.
- Once it is hot, stir in chopped onion then sautés until wilted and aromatic.
- Add sliced chorizo into the skillet then sauté until wilted.
- Transfer the lentils to the skillet then pour vegetable broth into it.
- Drizzle lemon juice and honey over the lentils then stir in mashed tomato into the lentils.
- Season with pepper and cook for about 5 minutes.
- Add bay leaf into the skillet and continue cooking until the gravy is thickened.
- Transfer to a serving dish then enjoy!

30 DAY PULSES CHALLENGE

Day 6

Breakfast : Nutritious Mung Beans Milk
Lunch : Green Peas Pasta
Dinner : Kidney Beans Soup with Beef

Nutritious Mung Beans Milk

Serving: 6

Nutrition Facts
Servings: 4
Per Serving
Calories 197
Total Fat 0.6g
Saturated Fat 0.2g
Trans Fat 0g
Cholesterol 0mg
Sodium 14mg
Potassium 653mg
Total Carb 36.8g
Dietary Fiber 8.4g
Sugars 7.8g
Protein 12.4g
Nutrition Facts
Servings: 4
Per Serving
Calories 197

Ingredients:

1 cup uncooked Mung beans

3 cups water

2 tablespoons brown sugar

30 DAY PULSES CHALLENGE

Directions:

- Wash and rinse the Mung beans then place in a bowl with a lid.
- Pour water to cover the beans then soak for at least 8 hours.
- After 8 discard the water then place the beans in a blender.
- Pour 3 cups water into the blender then blend until incorporated.
- Strain the milk then pour the milk into a pot then bring to boil.
- Once it is boiled, stir in brown sugar and stir well until the brown sugar is completely dissolved.
- Transfer the Mung beans milk to glasses.
- Serve and enjoy immediately.

30 DAY PULSES CHALLENGE

Green Peas Pasta

Serving: 3

Nutrition Facts
Servings: 3
Per Serving
Calories 175
Total Fat 6.7g
Saturated Fat 1.5g
Trans Fat 0g
Cholesterol 125mg
Sodium 50mg
Potassium 215mg
Total Carb 20.2g
Dietary Fiber 2.7g
Sugars 3.4g
Protein 8.9g
Nutrition Facts
Servings 3
Per Serving
Calories 175

Ingredients:

- 1 cup frozen green peas
- ½ cup uncooked pasta
- 2 organic eggs
- 2 teaspoons olive oil
- 1 teaspoon minced garlic
- ¼ cup chopped onion
- ¼ teaspoon pepper

Directions:

30 DAY PULSES CHALLENGE

- Cook the pasta according to its direction. Set aside.
- Pour water in a pot then bring to boil.
- Once it is boiled, place the green peas in the pot then cooks for 2 minutes until tender. Set aside.
- Preheat a skillet over medium heat then pour olive oil into it.
- Once it is hot, stir in chopped onion and minced garlic then sauté until wilted and aromatic.
- Add the steamed green peas and cooked pasta into the skillet then dust pepper on top. Sauté until both peas and pasta are completely seasoned.
- Crack the eggs then place in a bowl. Using a whisker, whisk the eggs until beaten.
- Pour the beaten eggs into the skillet then quickly stirs until becoming scrambled.
- Transfer the scrambled lentils to a serving dish then sprinkles pepper on top.
- Serve and enjoy.

30 DAY PULSES CHALLENGE

Kidney Beans and Beef Soup

Serving: 4

Nutrition Facts
Servings: 4
Per Serving
Calories 176
Total Fat 2.3g
Saturated Fat 0.6g
Trans Fat 0g
Cholesterol 6mg
Sodium 792mg
Potassium 707mg
Total Carb 24g
Dietary Fiber 5.5g
Sugars 1.7g
Protein 15g
Nutrition Facts
Servings: 4
Per Serving
Calories 176

Ingredients:

¾ cup cooked kidney beans

½ cup beef chunks

2 tablespoons sliced shallots

½ teaspoon pepper

¼ teaspoon nutmeg

2 cloves

¼ cup chopped leek

4 cups low sodium beef broth

Directions:

30 DAY PULSES CHALLENGE

- Place the beef chunks in a pressure cooker then process according its direction until the beef is tender. Set aside.
- Prepare a pot then place the cooked beans into it.
- Add beef into the pot then pours low sodium beef broth into the pot.
- Season with sliced shallot, pepper, cloves, and nutmeg then bring to boil.
- Once it is boiled, reduce the heat and cook for about 15 minutes.
- Transfer the kidney beans and beef soup to a bowl then serve warm.
- Best to be enjoyed in a cold winter night.

30 DAY PULSES CHALLENGE

Day 7

Breakfast : Green Peas Cabbage Salads
Lunch : Savory Lentils in Coconut Cream
Dinner : White Beans in Red

Green Peas Cabbage Salads

Serving: 2

Nutrition Facts
Servings: 2
Per Serving
Calories 92
Total Fat 2.8g
Saturated Fat 0.5g
Trans Fat 0g
Cholesterol 0mg
Sodium 11mg
Potassium 276mg
Total Carb 13.4g
Dietary Fiber 4.7g
Sugars 5.5g
Protein 4.6g
Nutrition Facts
Servings: 2
Per Serving
Calories 92

Ingredients:

1-cup green peas

¾ cup shredded cabbage

30 DAY PULSES CHALLENGE

½ cup sliced cucumber

1 tablespoon lemon juice

1-teaspoon olive oil

½ teaspoon pepper

Directions:

- Pour water in a pot then bring to boil.
- Once it is boiled, place the green peas in the pot then cooks for 2 minutes until tender.
- Transfer the green peas to a salad bowl then add shredded cabbage and sliced cucumber into the bowl.
- Splash lemon juice and olive oil over the salads then sprinkles pepper on top.
- Using two forks, toss the salads until combined.
- Serve and enjoy immediately.

30 DAY PULSES CHALLENGE

Savory Lentils in Coconut Cream

Serving: 8

Nutrition Facts
Servings: 8
Per Serving
Calories 229
Total Fat 14.7g
Saturated Fat 7.4g
Trans Fat 0g
Cholesterol 0mg
Sodium 7mg
Potassium 324mg
Total Carb 19g
Dietary Fiber 8.2g
Sugars 1.8g
Protein 7.2g
Nutrition Facts
Servings: 8
Per Serving
Calories 229

Ingredients:

4 tablespoons olive oil

1-cup cooked lentils

4 tablespoons chopped onion

2 tablespoons chopped leek

1 teaspoon minced garlic

¼ teaspoon cumin

1-teaspoon sesame seeds

2 tablespoons rice flour

1-cup coconut milk

Directions:

- Place lentils in a food processor together with minced garlic and cumin.
- Process until smooth then transfers to a bowl.
- Add chopped onion and leek into the bowl then using your hand, mix until combined.
- Shape into medium patties then roll into over the sesame seeds.
- Preheat a pan over medium heat then pours olive oil into it.
- Once it is hot, place the patties on the pan then fry until brown.
- Flip the patties and continue frying until both sides are brown.
- Strain from the oil then arrange on a serving dish.
- Pour half of the coconut milk into a saucepan then bring to boil.
- Meanwhile, combine rice flour with the remaining coconut milk then stirs until incorporated.
- When the coconut milk is boiled, stir in the rice flour mixture and stir vigorously.
- Once the sauce is thickened, transfer to a bowl then serve with the lentils patties.
- Enjoy warm!

30 DAY PULSES CHALLENGE

White Beans in Red

Serving: 4

Nutrition Facts
Servings: 4
Per Serving
Calories 232
Total Fat 3.1g
Saturated Fat 0.5g
Trans Fat 0g
Cholesterol 0mg
Sodium 318mg
Potassium 1168mg
Total Carb 41g
Dietary Fiber 9.2g
Sugars 6.5g
Protein 13.1g
Nutrition Facts
Servings: 4
Per Serving
Calories 232

Ingredients:

1 cup dried white beans

3 cups water

2 teaspoons olive oil

2 tablespoons chopped red pepper

½ cup chopped tomato

2 tablespoons tomato paste

1 teaspoon minced garlic

½ teaspoon pepper

¼ teaspoon ginger

¼ teaspoon nutmeg

61

30 DAY PULSES CHALLENGE

1 tablespoon chopped celery

3 cups low sodium vegetable broth

Directions:

- Wash and rinse the white beans then place in a bowl with a lid.
- Pour water to cover the white beans then soak for at least 8 hours.
- After 8 hours, pour water into a pot then bring to boil.
- Once it is boiled, strain the white beans then add into the hot water.
- Reduce the heat and bring to a simmer for about an hour.
- Strain the cooked white beans then set aside.
- Preheat a skillet over medium heat then pour olive oil into it.
- Once it is hot, stir in minced garlic then sautés until wilted and aromatic.
- Add tomato paste, chopped tomato and the cooked white beans.
- Season with pepper, nutmeg, ginger, red bell pepper, and lemon juice then sauté until the white beans are completely seasoned.
- Pour the vegetable broth and stir occasionally.
- Transfer the cooked beans to serving bowl then sprinkles chopped celery.
- Serve and enjoy!

30 DAY PULSES CHALLENGE

Day 8

Breakfast : Green Peas Omelets
Lunch : Chickpeas Tomato Salads
Dinner : Lentils Slices with Sweet Potato

Green Peas Omelets

Serving: 2

Nutrition Facts
Servings: 2
Per Serving
Calories 190
Total Fat 9.7g
Saturated Fat 2.5g
Trans Fat 0g
Cholesterol 169mg
Sodium 184mg
Potassium 341mg
Total Carb 17.7g
Dietary Fiber 3.1g
Sugars 3.9g
Protein 10.8g
Nutrition Facts
Servings: 2
Per Serving
Calories 190

Ingredients:

1-teaspoon olive oil

2 organic eggs

¼ teaspoon pepper

¼ cup frozen green peas

1-tablespoon corn kernels

½ tablespoon chopped bacon

Directions:

- Pour water in a pot then bring to boil.
- Once it is boiled, place the green peas in the pot then cooks for 2 minutes until tender. Set aside.
- Preheat a saucepan over medium heat.
- Crack the eggs then place in a bowl.
- Season with pepper then add peas, corn kernels, and bacon into the eggs. Mix well.
- Preheat a small frying pan over medium heat then pour olive oil into it.
- Once it is hot, pour the egg mixture into the pan and tilt to spread out the egg.
- Cook until the omelet is set then transfer to a serving dish.
- Enjoy!

30 DAY PULSES CHALLENGE

Chickpeas Tomato Salads

Serving: 4

Nutrition Facts
Servings: 4
Per Serving
Calories 223
Total Fat 6.7g
Saturated Fat 0.9g
Trans Fat 0g
Cholesterol 0mg
Sodium 22mg
Potassium 531mg
Total Carb 32.5g
Dietary Fiber 9.1g
Sugars 6.2g
Protein 10.1g
Nutrition Facts
Servings: 4
Per Serving
Calories 223

Ingredients:

1 cup dried chickpeas

3 teaspoons olive oil

2 tablespoons chopped celery

½ cup diced tomato

½ teaspoon black pepper

2 tablespoons lemon juice

2 tablespoons chopped shallot

2 cups water

Directions:

- Wash and rinse the chickpeas then place in a bowl with a lid.
- Pour water to cover the chickpeas then soak overnight.
- In the morning, pour water into a pot then bring to boil.
- Once it is boiled, strain the chickpeas then add into the hot water.
- Reduce the heat and bring to a simmer for about an hour.
- Strain the cooked chickpeas then transfers to a salad bowl.
- Add chopped celery, chopped shallot, and diced tomato into the bowl.
- Sprinkle black pepper over the chickpeas then drizzle lemon juice and olive oil on top.
- Toss until combined then enjoy!

30 DAY PULSES CHALLENGE

Lentils Slices with Sweet Potato

Serving: 4

Nutrition Facts
Servings: 6
Per Serving
Calories 239
Total Fat 9.9g
Saturated Fat 5g
Trans Fat 0g
Cholesterol 0mg
Sodium 33mg
Potassium 471mg
Total Carb 29.7g
Dietary Fiber 11.3g
Sugars 3.6g
Protein 9.7g
Nutrition Facts
Servings: 6
Per Serving
Calories 239

Ingredients:

1-½ cups cooked lentils

½ cup chopped green beans

¾ cup mashed sweet potato

¼ cup chopped onion

¼ cup diced carrots

2 teaspoons minced garlic

½ cup coconut milk

2 tablespoons olive oil

1-teaspoon liquid smoke

¼ teaspoon pepper

Directions:

- Preheat an oven to 375 F then coats a medium loaf pan with cooking oil. Set aside.
- Place lentils in a food processor together with onion, olive oil, minced garlic, liquid smoke, pepper, and coconut milk. Process until smooth.
- Transfer the smooth lentils to a bowl then add green beans, mashed sweet potato, and diced carrot.
- Using your hand, mix until combined then transfer to the prepared loaf pan. Spread evenly.
- Bake for 30 minutes until the top is lightly brown.
- Once it is done, remove from the oven then place on a serving dish. Let it cool for a few minutes.
- Cut the loaf into slices then serve.

30 DAY PULSES CHALLENGE

Day 9

Breakfast : Nutritious Green Peas Salads
Lunch : Beans Burrito with Peanut Sauce
Dinner : Lentils Turmeric Soup

Nutritious Green Peas Salads

Serving: 2

Nutrition Facts
Servings: 2
Per Serving
Calories 135
Total Fat 1.6g
Saturated Fat 0.4g
Trans Fat 0g
Cholesterol 3mg
Sodium 66mg
Potassium 400mg
Total Carb 22.2g
Dietary Fiber 7.9g
Sugars 8.8g
Protein 9g
Nutrition Facts
Servings: 2
Per Serving
Calories 135

Ingredients:

2 cups green peas

¼ cup sliced bacon

½ cup chopped cabbage

30 DAY PULSES CHALLENGE

¼ teaspoon pepper

Directions:

- Place the green peas in a steamer then steam for 2 minutes until tender. Set aside.
- Preheat a saucepan over medium heat.
- Once it is hot, stir in the sliced bacon then sautés until crispy.
- Add the green peas into the saucepan then seasons with pepper.
- Arrange the raw cabbage on a serving platter.
- Place the green peas and bacon over the cabbage.
- Serve and enjoy immediately.

30 DAY PULSES CHALLENGE

Beans Burrito with Peanut Sauce

Serving: 4

Nutrition Facts
Servings: 4
Per Serving
Calories 145
Total Fat 4.1g
Saturated Fat 0.6g
Trans Fat 0g
Cholesterol 0mg
Sodium 466mg
Potassium 165mg
Total Carb 25.4g
Dietary Fiber 3g
Sugars 12g
Protein 3.6g
Nutrition Facts
Servings: 4
Per Serving
Calories 145

Ingredients:

1 cup cooked beans

2 tablespoons chopped onion

2 tablespoons soy sauce

2 tablespoons brown sugar

1-teaspoon olive oil

2 tablespoons chopped peanut

2 tablespoons tamarind water

4 tortillas

Directions:

- Preheat a skillet over medium heat then pour olive oil into it.
- Once it is hot, stir in chopped onion then sautés until wilted and aromatic.
- Add beans into the skillet together with half of soy sauce and brown sugar. Stir well.
- Remove from heat then let it cool.
- After that, place chopped cashew in a food processor then add the remaining soy sauce and brown sugar.
- Pour tamarind water into the food processor then process until incorporated.
- Place the tortillas on a flat surface.
- Drop the filling mixture on each tortilla then roll each tortilla tightly.
- Arrange on a serving dish then drizzle cashew sauce on top.
- Serve and enjoy immediately.

30 DAY PULSES CHALLENGE

Lentils Turmeric Soup

Serving: 4

Nutrition Facts
Servings: 4
Per Serving
Calories 196
Total Fat 2.3g
Saturated Fat 0.4g
Trans Fat 0g
Cholesterol 0mg
Sodium 199mg
Potassium 476mg
Total Carb 31.6g
Dietary Fiber 14.8g
Sugars 1.6g
Protein 12.5g
Nutrition Facts
Servings 4
Per Serving
Calories 196

Ingredients:

1 cup uncooked lentils

1 ½ teaspoons olive oil

1 teaspoon minced garlic

1 teaspoon sliced shallot

¼ teaspoon turmeric

¼ teaspoon bay leaf

1 tablespoon lemon juice

¼ teaspoon cumin

2 cups low sodium vegetable broth

¼ teaspoon pepper

30 DAY PULSES CHALLENGE

Directions:

- Preheat olive oil in a pot over medium heat.
- Stir in minced garlic and sliced shallot then sauté until wilted and aromatic.
- Add cumin, turmeric, and bay leaf into the pot then cook for about 2 minutes.
- Next, stir in lentils then pour vegetable broth into the pot. Bring to boil.
- Once it is boil, season with pepper and lemon juice then covers the pot with the lid. Reduce the heat.
- Cook for about 30 minutes until the lentils are tender.
- Transfer to a soup bowl and enjoy warm.

30 DAY PULSES CHALLENGE

Day 10

Breakfast : Nutritious Mashed Lentils
Lunch : Delicious Red Beans Fritter
Dinner : Sautéed Kidney Beans with Carrot

Nutritious Mashed Lentils

Serving: 4

Nutrition Facts
Servings: 4
Per Serving
Calories 228
Total Fat 6.5g
Saturated Fat 3.8g
Trans Fat 0g
Cholesterol 16mg
Sodium 49mg
Potassium 476mg
Total Carb 30.1g
Dietary Fiber 14.8g
Sugars 1.5g
Protein 12.8g
Nutrition Facts
Servings: 4
Per Serving
Calories 228

Ingredients:

1 cup uncooked lentils

2 tablespoons butter

2 tablespoons milk

¼ teaspoon pepper

¼ cup chopped leek

Directions:

- Place lentils in a pot then pour water over the lentils. Bring to boil.
- Once it is boil, covers the pot with the lid then reduces the heat.
- Cook for about 30 minutes until the lentils are tender.
- Strain the lentils then place in a food processor.
- Add butter and leek then dust pepper on top.
- Pour milk over the lentils then process until smooth and creamy.
- Transfer to a serving dish then enjoys immediately.

30 DAY PULSES CHALLENGE

Delicious Beans Fritter

Serving: 4

Nutrition Facts
Servings: 4
Per Serving
Calories 271
Total Fat 13.1g
Saturated Fat 1.9g
Trans Fat 0g
Cholesterol 0mg
Sodium 7mg
Potassium 650mg
Total Carb 30g
Dietary Fiber 7.3g
Sugars 1.5g
Protein 10.6g
Nutrition Facts
Servings: 4
Per Serving
Calories 271

Ingredients:

¼ cup olive oil

1 cup cooked beans

¼ cup chopped onion

¼ cup chopped leek

1 teaspoon minced garlic

¼ teaspoon black pepper

Directions:

- Place the cooked red beans in a food processor together with chopped onion, chopped parsley, minced garlic, and black

pepper. Process until incorporated and smooth.
- Shape the mixture into small patties form then chill in the refrigerator for 10 minutes.
- Preheat a non-stick pan over medium heat then pour olive oil into it.
- Take the patties out from the refrigerator then place in the pan.
- Fry for about 3 minutes until brown then flips and cook for another 3 minutes until both sides of the fritters are brown.
- Once it is done, transfer to a serving dish. Enjoy!

30 DAY PULSES CHALLENGE

Sautéed Kidney Beans with Carrots

Serving: 4

Nutrition Facts
Servings: 4
Per Serving
Calories 179
Total Fat 2.8g
Saturated Fat 0.4g
Trans Fat 0g
Cholesterol 0mg
Sodium 6mg
Potassium 637mg
Total Carb 29.1g
Dietary Fiber 7.1g
Sugars 1g
Protein 10.5g
Nutrition Facts
Servings: 4
Per Serving
Calories 179

Ingredients:

- 2 teaspoons olive oil
- ½ cup cooked kidney beans
- ¼ cup shredded carrot
- ¼ cup chopped onion
- ½ teaspoon pepper

Directions:

- Preheat a skillet over medium heat then pour olive oil into it.

30 DAY PULSES CHALLENGE

- Once it is hot, stir in chopped onion then sautés until wilted and aromatic.
- Add the cooked kidney beans and shredded carrot then season with pepper.
- Stirring occasionally and cook until the beans and carrot are completely seasoned and tender.
- Transfer to a serving dish then enjoy!

30 DAY PULSES CHALLENGE

Day 11

Breakfast : White Beans Crumbles with Peas and Cheese
Lunch : Natural Sweet Beans Salads
Dinner : Chickpeas Curry with Cabbage

White Beans Crumbles with Peas and Cheese

Serving: 4

Nutrition Facts
Servings: 4
Per Serving
Calories 183
Total Fat 3.9g
Saturated Fat 2.3g
Trans Fat 0g
Cholesterol 12mg
Sodium 78mg
Potassium 405mg
Total Carb 28.5g
Dietary Fiber 4.4g
Sugars 12.9g
Protein 10g
Nutrition Facts
Servings: 4
Per Serving
Calories 183

Ingredients:

½ cup uncooked kidney beans

1-½ cups water

½ cup steamed peas

¼ cup grated cheese

2 tablespoons raw honey

1-cup milk

Directions:

- Wash and rinse the kidney beans then place in a container with a lid.
- Pour water to cover the beans then covers the container with the lid and soaks the beans overnight.
- In the morning, rinse and strain the beans.
- Pour 1-½ cups of water into a pot then bring to boil.
- Once it is boiled, stir in the kidney beans then cook for an hour.
- Strain the cooked kidney beans then place in a food processor. Process the cooked beans until smooth.
- Transfer the beans crumbles to a serving bowl.
- Add steamed peas into the bowl then pour milk over the crumbled beans. Using a spoon, mix until combined—it is like making oats in a bowl.
- Drizzle honey and sprinkle grated cheese on top then serve immediately.

30 DAY PULSES CHALLENGE

Natural Sweet Beans Salads

Serving: 4

Nutrition Facts
Servings: 6
Per Serving
Calories 230
Total Fat 13.2g
Saturated Fat 8.9g
Trans Fat 0g
Cholesterol 0mg
Sodium 18mg
Potassium 419mg
Total Carb 23.3g
Dietary Fiber 7g
Sugars 5.1g
Protein 7.5g
Nutrition Facts
Servings: 6
Per Serving
Calories 230

Ingredients:

1 cup cooked black beans

1 cup cooked white beans

2 tablespoons chopped shallot

2 tablespoons chopped celery

2 tablespoons raw honey

1 tablespoon lemon juice

Directions:

- Place the beans in a salad bowl.
- Add chopped shallot and celery into the bowl.

30 DAY PULSES CHALLENGE

- Drizzle raw honey and splash lemon juice on top.
- Using 2 forks mix the beans until combined.
- Serve and enjoy.
- If you want to consume it later, store in a refrigerator and enjoy anytime you want.

30 DAY PULSES CHALLENGE

Chickpeas Curry with Cabbage

Serving: 4

Nutrition Facts
Servings: 6
Per Serving
Calories 230
Total Fat 13.2g
Saturated Fat 8.9g
Trans Fat 0g
Cholesterol 0mg
Sodium 18mg
Potassium 419mg
Total Carb 23.3g
Dietary Fiber 7g
Sugars 5.1g
Protein 7.5g
Nutrition Facts
Servings: 6
Per Serving
Calories 230

Ingredients:

1 cup dried chickpeas

2 teaspoons olive oil

½ cup chopped cabbage

1 teaspoon minced garlic

1 teaspoon sliced shallot

½ teaspoon curry powder

½ teaspoon candlenut powder

½ teaspoon pepper

1 tablespoon chopped celery

1-cup water

30 DAY PULSES CHALLENGE

1-cup coconut milk

Directions:

- Wash and rinse the chickpeas then place in a bowl with a lid.
- Pour water to cover the chickpeas then soak overnight.
- In the morning, pour water into a pot then bring to boil.
- Once it is boiled, strain the chickpeas then add into the hot water.
- Reduce the heat and bring to a simmer for about an hour.
- Strain the cooked chickpeas then set aside.
- Preheat a skillet over medium heat then pour olive oil into it.
- Once it is hot, stir in minced garlic and sliced shallot then sauté until wilted and aromatic.
- Add candlenut powder, curry powder, and pepper into the skillet then stir in the cooked chickpeas. Sauté until the chickpeas are completely seasoned.
- Pour water and coconut milk then stir occasionally.
- Once the curry is completely boiled, stir in chopped cabbage.
- Transfer the chickpeas curry to a serving bowl then sprinkles chopped celery.
- Serve and enjoy!

30 DAY PULSES CHALLENGE

30 DAY PULSES CHALLENGE

Day 12

Breakfast : Nutritious Chickpeas, Green Peas, and Beef
Lunch : Green Peas Crispy Samosa
Dinner : Baked Lentils with Cheese

Nutritious Chickpeas, Green Peas, and Beef

Serving: 4

Nutrition Facts
Servings: 4
Per Serving
Calories 279
Total Fat 5.8g
Saturated Fat 1.1g
Trans Fat 0g
Cholesterol 10mg
Sodium 467mg
Potassium 644mg
Total Carb 41.3g
Dietary Fiber 11g
Sugars 10g
Protein 16.6g
Nutrition Facts
Servings: 4
Per Serving
Calories 279

Ingredients:

1 cup cooked chickpeas

1 cup cooked green peas

½ cup sliced beef

½ cup cubed potato

1 teaspoon minced garlic

1 teaspoon sliced shallots

1-tablespoon soy sauce

1-tablespoon brown sugar

1-cup low sodium beef broth

1-teaspoon olive oil

Directions:

- Preheat a skillet over medium heat then pour olive oil into it.
- Once it is hot, stir in minced garlic and sliced shallot then sautés until wilted and aromatic.
- Add beef into the skillet then sautés until the beef is no longer pink.
- Add green peas, chickpeas, and potatoes then pour beef broth into the skillet.
- Stir well then bring to boil.
- Once it is boiled, reduce the heat and continue cooking until the beef broth is reduced into half.
- Add soy sauce and brown sugar then stir well.
- Transfer to a serving dish then enjoy!

30 DAY PULSES CHALLENGE

Green Peas Samosa

Serving: 4

Nutrition Facts
Servings: 4
Per Serving
Calories 210
Total Fat 6.8g
Saturated Fat 1g
Trans Fat 0g
Cholesterol 0mg
Sodium 234mg
Potassium 69mg
Total Carb 34.8g
Dietary Fiber 2.2g
Sugars 2.5g
Protein 5.1g
Nutrition Facts
Servings: 4
Per Serving
Calories 210

Ingredients:

2 teaspoons olive oil

½ cup cooked green peas

2 tablespoons diced carrot

¼ cup chopped onion

½ teaspoon pepper

4 pastry sheets

Vegetable oil, to fry

Directions:

30 DAY PULSES CHALLENGE

- Preheat a skillet over medium heat then pour olive oil into it.
- Once it is hot, stir in chopped onion then sautés until wilted and aromatic.
- Add the green peas and diced carrots then season with pepper.
- Stirring occasionally and cook until the peas and carrot are completely seasoned and tender.
- Place the pastry sheets on a flat surface then drop about 2 tablespoons of the filling.
- Fold the tortillas into triangles; make sure to tighten the samosa.
- Pour vegetable oil in a saucepan over medium heat.
- Once it is hot, stir in the samosas then fry until lightly brown.
- Flip the samosas then continue frying until all of the samosa's sides are lightly brown.
- Strain the oil then serve warm.

30 DAY PULSES CHALLENGE

Baked Lentils with Cheese

Serving: 6

Nutrition Facts
Servings: 6
Per Serving
Calories 221
Total Fat 8.5g
Saturated Fat 3.1g
Trans Fat 0g
Cholesterol 10mg
Sodium 47mg
Potassium 387mg
Total Carb 23.8g
Dietary Fiber 11.7g
Sugars 1.2g
Protein 12.8g
Nutrition Facts
Servings: 6
Per Serving
Calories 221

Ingredients:

½ lb. uncooked lentils

¼ cup chopped onion

1-teaspoon minced garlic

1 bay leaf

2 tablespoons chopped parsley

1-½ cups water

2 tablespoons goat cheese

2 tablespoons vinegar

1 teaspoon Dijon mustard

2 tablespoons olive oil

Directions:

- Place lentils in a pot together onion, minced garlic, bay leaf, and chopped parsley.
- Pour water over the lentils then bring to boil.
- Once it is boil, covers the pot with the lid then reduces the heat.
- Cook for about 30 minutes until the lentils are tender.
- Preheat an oven to 350 F then coat a baking dish with cooking spray
- Strain the lentils then transfer to the prepared baking dish.
- Add vinegar, Dijon mustard, and olive oil into the dish then pours about ½ cup of liquid from the lentils. Mix until combined.
- Top with cheese then bake for about 15 minutes until the cheese has softened.
- Transfer to a serving dish and enjoy warm.

30 DAY PULSES CHALLENGE

Day 13

Breakfast : Green Feta Salads
Lunch : Tasty Lentils Burger
Dinner : Savory Mixed Beans Stew

Green Feta Salads

Serving: 2

Nutrition Facts
Servings: 2
Per Serving
Calories 211
Total Fat 8.7g
Saturated Fat 3.4g
Trans Fat 0g
Cholesterol 17mg
Sodium 225mg
Potassium 625mg
Total Carb 20.1g
Dietary Fiber 6.4g
Sugars 5g
Protein 15.2g
Nutrition Facts
Servings: 2
Per Serving
Calories 211

Ingredients:

1-cup green peas

½ cup edamame

¼ cup Feta cheese

30 DAY PULSES CHALLENGE

2 tablespoons sliced shallot

2 teaspoons lemon juice

Directions:

- Pour water in a pot then bring to boil.
- Once it is boiled, place the green peas in the pot then cooks for 2 minutes until tender.
- Once it is done, transfer to a salad bowl then add sliced shallots and lemon juice over the peas. Toss to combine.
- After that, sprinkle Feta cheese on top then enjoy right away.

30 DAY PULSES CHALLENGE

Tasty Lentils Burger

Serving: 4

Nutrition Facts
Servings: 4
Per Serving
Calories 345
Total Fat 4.4g
Saturated Fat 0.4g
Trans Fat 0g
Cholesterol 0mg
Sodium 777mg
Potassium 521mg
Total Carb 59.7g
Dietary Fiber 20g
Sugars 4.6g
Protein 19.4g
Nutrition Facts
Servings: 4
Per Serving
Calories 345

Ingredients:

1 cup cooked lentils

2 teaspoons olive oil

1 teaspoon minced garlic

1 teaspoon sliced shallot

1 bay leaf

¼ cup low sodium soy sauce

¼ cup chopped tomato

1-cup water

1-teaspoon cornstarch

4 whole-wheat buns

Directions:

- Preheat a skillet over medium heat then pour olive oil into it.
- Once it is hot, stir in minced garlic, sliced shallot, and bay leaf then sauté until wilted and aromatic.
- Add lentils and chopped tomato into the skillet then drizzle soy sauce on top.
- Sauté until wilted then pour water into the skillet. Cook for a few minutes until the water is completely absorbed.
- Take a spoonful of gravy then combine with cornstarch. Mix until incorporated.
- Bring to a simmer for about 30 seconds then remove from heat.
- Horizontally cut the buns into halves then fill with the lentils.
- Enjoy your tasty lunch!

30 DAY PULSES CHALLENGE

Original Mixed Beans Stew

Serving: 4

Nutrition Facts
Servings: 4
Per Serving
Calories 203
Total Fat 4.1g
Saturated Fat 0.7g
Trans Fat 0g
Cholesterol 0mg
Sodium 55mg
Potassium 752mg
Total Carb 31.8g
Dietary Fiber 7.6g
Sugars 1.8g
Protein 11g
Nutrition Facts
Servings: 4
Per Serving
Calories 203

Ingredients:

4 tablespoons cooked kidney beans

4 tablespoons cooked black beans

4 tablespoons cooked pinto beans

4 tablespoons cooked white beans

3 teaspoons olive oil

½ teaspoon ginger

1 teaspoon minced garlic

1 bay leaf

¼ teaspoon nutmeg

1 ½ teaspoons tamarind

½ cup low sodium vegetable broth

Directions:

- Preheat a skillet over medium heat then pour olive oil into it.
- Once it is hot, stir in minced garlic then sautés until wilted and aromatic.
- Add the cooked kidney beans then seasons with ginger, bay leaf, and tamarind.
- Stirring occasionally and cook until the beans are completely seasoned.
- Pour vegetable broth into the skillet then bring to boil.
- Once it is boiled, reduce the heat and continue cooking until the gravy is thickened.
- Transfer to a serving dish then enjoy warm.

Day 14

Breakfast : Healthy Cannellini Beans with Spinach
Lunch : Spicy Lentils and Peas Balls
Dinner : Inspired Lentils with Pork and Quinoa

Healthy Cannellini Beans with Spinach

Serving: 2

Nutrition Facts
Servings: 2
Per Serving
Calories 202
Total Fat 5.1g
Saturated Fat 0.7g
Trans Fat 0g
Cholesterol 0mg
Sodium 16mg
Potassium 695mg
Total Carb 29.5g
Dietary Fiber 11.9g
Sugars 1.7g
Protein 11.2g
Nutrition Facts
Servings: 2
Per Serving
Calories 202

Ingredients:

2 teaspoons olive oil

½ cup uncooked Cannellini Beans

¼ cup chopped spinach

30 DAY PULSES CHALLENGE

¼ cup chopped onion

1 teaspoon minced garlic

¼ cup water

Directions:

- Wash and rinse the Cannellini beans then place in a container with a lid.
- Pour water to cover the beans then covers the container with the lid and soaks the beans overnight—3 cups water for 1-cup beans
- In the morning, rinse and strain the beans.
- Pour water into a pot then bring to boil.
- Once it is boiled, stir in the Cannellini beans then cook for an hour.
- Strain the cooked Cannellini beans then sets aside.
- Preheat a skillet over medium heat then pour olive oil into it.
- Once it is hot, stir in chopped onion and minced garlic then sautés until wilted and aromatic.
- Add the cooked beans and chopped spinach into the skillet. Stir well.
- Pour water into the skillet and cook until the beans and spinach are tender.
- Transfer to a serving dish then enjoy!

30 DAY PULSES CHALLENGE

Spicy Lentils and Peas Balls

Serving: 7

Nutrition Facts
Servings: 4
Per Serving
Calories 297
Total Fat 13.2g
Saturated Fat 1.9g
Trans Fat 0g
Cholesterol 0mg
Sodium 4mg
Potassium 521mg
Total Carb 32.5g
Dietary Fiber 15.8g
Sugars 2.4g
Protein 13.5g
Nutrition Facts
Servings: 4
Per Serving
Calories 297

Ingredients:

¼ cup olive oil

1 cup cooked lentils

½ cup cooked green peas

1-tablespoon chili flakes

¼ cup chopped onion

1 teaspoon minced garlic

¼ teaspoon black pepper

Directions:

- Place lentils and green peas in a bowl then add chili flakes, chopped onion, minced garlic, and black pepper.
- Using your hand, mix until combined and becoming dough.
- Shape the mixture into small balls form then chill in the refrigerator for 10 minutes.
- Preheat a non-stick pan over medium heat then pour olive oil into it.
- Take the patties out from the refrigerator then place in the pan.
- Fry for about 3 minutes until brown then flips and cook for another 3 minutes until both sides of the fritters are brown.
- Once it is done, transfer to a serving dish. Enjoy!

Inspired Lentils with Pork and Quinoa

Serving: 4

Nutrition Facts
Servings: 4
Per Serving
Calories 282
Total Fat 7.8g
Saturated Fat 2g
Trans Fat 0g
Cholesterol 8mg
Sodium 309mg
Potassium 642mg
Total Carb 36.5g
Dietary Fiber 16.4g
Sugars 1.6g
Protein 17.8g
Nutrition Facts
Servings: 4
Per Serving

30 DAY PULSES CHALLENGE

Calories 282

Ingredients:

1 cup cooked lentils

¼ lb. cooked pork chunks

3 tablespoons cooked quinoa

2 teaspoons olive oil

1 teaspoon minced garlic

1 teaspoon sliced shallot

1-teaspoon pepper

1-cup water

Directions:

- Preheat a skillet over medium heat then pour olive oil into it.
- Once it is hot, stir in minced garlic, sliced shallot, and bay leaf then sauté until wilted and aromatic.
- Add the pork chunks, quinoa, and lentils into the skillet then season with pepper.
- Sauté until all of the ingredients are completely seasoned then transfers to a serving dish.
- Enjoy!

Day 15

30 DAY PULSES CHALLENGE

Breakfast : Chickpeas Egg Porridge
Lunch : Black-eyed Peas Salads with Zucchini
Dinner : Kidney Beans Garlic

Chickpeas Egg Porridge

Serving: 4

Nutrition Facts
Servings: 4
Per Serving
Calories 239
Total Fat 7.6g
Saturated Fat 1.3g
Trans Fat 0g
Cholesterol 82mg
Sodium 50mg
Potassium 489mg
Total Carb 31.8g
Dietary Fiber 9g
Sugars 5.8g
Protein 12.6g
Nutrition Facts
Servings: 4
Per Serving
Calories 239

Ingredients:

1 cup dried chickpeas

2 organic eggs

2 teaspoons olive oil

1 teaspoon minced garlic

½ teaspoon curry powder

30 DAY PULSES CHALLENGE

½ teaspoon pepper

¼ cup chopped leek

3 cups water

Directions:

- Wash and rinse the chickpeas then place in a bowl with a lid.
- Pour water to cover the chickpeas then soak overnight.
- In the morning, pour water into a pot then bring to boil.
- Once it is boiled, strain the chickpeas then add into the hot water.
- Reduce the heat and bring to a simmer for about an hour.
- Strain the cooked chickpeas then set aside.
- Preheat a skillet over medium heat then pours olive oil into it.
- Once it is hot, stir in minced garlic then sauté until wilted and aromatic.
- Add curry powder and pepper into the skillet then stir in the cooked chickpeas. Sauté until the chickpeas are completely seasoned.
- Pour the chickpeas liquid then stir occasionally.
- Once it is done, remove from the heat then using n immersion blender, blend until smooth.
- Place the eggs in a bowl then using a whisker, whisk until just beaten.
- Return the smooth chickpeas to the heat and bring to boil.

30 DAY PULSES CHALLENGE

- Once it is boiled, drizzle the beaten eggs over the porridge and stir vigorously until the eggs are completely dissolved with the porridge.
- Transfer the porridge to a serving bowl then sprinkles chopped leek on top.
- Serve and enjoy warm.

30 DAY PULSES CHALLENGE

Black-eyed Peas Salads with Zucchini

Serving: 4

Nutrition Facts
Servings: 2
Per Serving
Calories 187
Total Fat 8.4g
Saturated Fat 1.2g
Trans Fat 0g
Cholesterol 0mg
Sodium 45mg
Potassium 526mg
Total Carb 23.6g
Dietary Fiber 6g
Sugars 2.9g
Protein 7.9g
Nutrition Facts
Servings: 2
Per Serving
Calories 187

Ingredients:

- 1 cup dried black-eyed peas
- 3 teaspoons olive oil
- ½ cup cubed zucchini
- ¼ cup cooked corn kernels
- 2 tablespoons diced tomato
- 2 tablespoons sliced onion
- 2 tablespoons lemon juice
- 3 cups water

30 DAY PULSES CHALLENGE

Directions:

- Wash and rinse the black-eyed peas then place in a bowl with a lid.
- Pour water to cover the peas then soak overnight—3 cups water for 1-cup peas.
- In the morning, pour water into a pot then bring to boil.
- Once it is boiled, strain the black-eyed peas then add into the hot water.
- Reduce the heat and bring to a simmer for about an hour.
- Strain the cooked black-eyed peas then transfers to a salad bowl.
- Add cubed zucchini, corn kernels, tomato, and sliced onion into the bowl.
- Drizzle lemon juice and olive oil on top the toss until combined.
- Serve and enjoy!

30 DAY PULSES CHALLENGE

Kidney Beans Garlic

Serving: 4

Nutrition Facts
Servings: 4
Per Serving
Calories 179
Total Fat 2.8g
Saturated Fat 0.4g
Trans Fat 0g
Cholesterol 0mg
Sodium 6mg
Potassium 637mg
Total Carb 29.1g
Dietary Fiber 7.1g
Sugars 1g
Protein 10.5g
Nutrition Facts
Servings: 4
Per Serving
Calories 179

Ingredients:

2 teaspoons olive oil

1 cup uncooked kidney beans

3 teaspoons minced garlic

½ teaspoon pepper

Directions:

- Wash and rinse the kidney beans then place in a container with a lid.
- Pour water to cover the beans then covers the container with the lid and soaks the

- beans overnight—3 cups water for 1-cup beans.
- In the morning, rinse and strain the beans.
- Pour water into a pot then bring to boil.
- Once it is boiled, stir in the kidney beans then cook for an hour.
- Strain the cooked kidney beans then sets aside.
- Preheat a skillet over medium heat then pour olive oil into it.
- Once it is hot, stir in garlic then sautés until aromatic and lightly golden.
- Add the cooked kidney beans then season with pepper.
- Stirring occasionally and cook until the beans are completely seasoned.
- Transfer to a serving dish then enjoy!

Day 16

Breakfast : Lentils Porridge with Orange sauce
Lunch : Delicious Beans Pie
Dinner : Cannellini Mushroom Soup

Lentils Porridge with Orange Sauce

Serving: 4

30 DAY PULSES CHALLENGE

Nutrition Facts
Servings: 4
Per Serving
Calories 299
Total Fat 7.2g
Saturated Fat 4.4g
Trans Fat 0g
Cholesterol 19mg
Sodium 282mg
Potassium 727mg
Total Carb 41.6g
Dietary Fiber 14.8g
Sugars 11g
Protein 16.4g
Nutrition Facts
Servings: 4
Per Serving
Calories 299

Ingredients:

- 1 cup uncooked lentils
- 2 cups low sodium vegetable broth
- 1 cup orange juice
- 1-cup yogurt
- 2 tablespoons butter

Directions:

- Place lentils in a pot then pour water over the lentils.
- Let the lentils sit for almost an hour then strains the lentils.
- Transfer to a food processor then process until becoming crumbled.
- After that, place the lentils in a pot then pour vegetable oil on top. Bring to boil.

- Once it is boiled, reduce the heat then continue cooking until the broth is completely absorbed.
- Place the cooked lentils in a bowl then quickly stir in butter—while the lentils are still hot. Set aside.
- Next, combine orange juice and yogurt then mix until incorporated.
- Drizzle the orange yogurt over the lentils then serve immediately.

30 DAY PULSES CHALLENGE

Delicious Beans Pie

Serving: 4

Nutrition Facts
Servings: 6
Per Serving
Calories 239
Total Fat 9.9g
Saturated Fat 5g
Trans Fat 0g
Cholesterol 0mg
Sodium 33mg
Potassium 471mg
Total Carb 29.7g
Dietary Fiber 11.3g
Sugars 3.6g
Protein 9.7g
Nutrition Facts
Servings: 6
Per Serving
Calories 239

Ingredients:

1-½ cups cooked Mung beans

¼ cup chopped grated carrot

¾ cup mashed sweet potato

1 organic egg white

¼ cup chopped onion

2 teaspoons minced garlic

3 tablespoons soymilk

2 tablespoons olive oil

¼ teaspoon pepper

30 DAY PULSES CHALLENGE

Directions:

- Preheat an oven to 375 F then lines a baking sheet with parchment paper. Set aside.
- Place Mung beans in a food processor together with onion, olive oil, minced garlic, pepper, and soymilk. Process until smooth.
- Transfer the smooth beans to a bowl then add mashed sweet potato, egg white, and grated carrot.
- Using your hand, mix until combined then drop a spoonful of mixture on the prepared baking sheet.
- Repeat with the remaining mixture and arranges them on the baking sheet.
- Bake for 30 minutes until the top is lightly brown.
- Take the beans pies out from the oven then arrange on a serving platter.
- Serve and enjoy warm.

30 DAY PULSES CHALLENGE

Cannellini Mushroom Soup

Serving: 4

Nutrition Facts
Servings: 4
Per Serving
Calories 179
Total Fat 0.7g
Saturated Fat 0.1g
Trans Fat 0g
Cholesterol 0mg
Sodium 19mg
Potassium 913mg
Total Carb 33g
Dietary Fiber 13.2g
Sugars 4.3g
Protein 12g
Nutrition Facts
Servings: 4
Per Serving
Calories 179

Ingredients:

1-cup cooked Cannellini beans

¼ cup chopped mushroom

2 large red tomatoes

¼ teaspoon nutmeg

¼ cup chopped onion

2 tablespoons red chili

½ teaspoon pepper

1-cup water

Directions:

30 DAY PULSES CHALLENGE

- Place tomatoes, red chili, nutmeg, and pepper in a blender.
- Pour water into the blender then blends until smooth and incorporated.
- Place cooked beans and mushroom into a pan then add chopped onion over the mushroom.
- Pour the tomato and chili mixture into the pan then bring to boil.
- Once it is boiled, reduce the heat and continue to cook for about 15 minutes.
- Transfer to a serving bowl then enjoy warm.

Day 17

Breakfast : Mung Beans Porridge with Coconut Milk
Lunch : Cheesy Black Beans in Wrap
Dinner : Lentils Stew with Green Peas

Mung Beans Porridge with Coconut Milk

Serving: 6

Nutrition Facts
Servings: 6
Per Serving
Calories 223
Total Fat 9.9g
Saturated Fat 8.6g

30 DAY PULSES CHALLENGE

Trans Fat 0g
Cholesterol 0mg
Sodium 16mg
Potassium 540mg
Total Carb 26.8g
Dietary Fiber 6.5g
Sugars 6.5g
Protein 9.2g
Nutrition Facts
Servings: 6
Per Serving
Calories 223

Ingredients:

1 cup uncooked Mung beans

3 cups water

2 tablespoons brown sugar

1-cup coconut milk

Directions:

- Wash and rinse the Mung beans then place in a bowl with a lid.
- Pour water to cover the beans then soak for at least 8 hours.
- After 8 hours, pour 3 cups water into a pot then bring to boil.
- Once it is boiled, strain the Mung beans then add into the hot water.
- Reduce the heat and bring to a simmer for about an hour.
- Add brown sugar into the pot and mix with the beans until the brown sugar is completely dissolved.
- Transfer the Mung beans porridge to a serving bowl then pour coconut milk n top.
- Serve and enjoy immediately.

30 DAY PULSES CHALLENGE

30 DAY PULSES CHALLENGE

Cheesy Black Beans in Wrap

Serving: 4

Nutrition Facts
Servings: 4
Per Serving
Calories 340
Total Fat 18.9g
Saturated Fat 10.2g
Trans Fat 0g
Cholesterol 39mg
Sodium 444mg
Potassium 377mg
Total Carb 36g
Dietary Fiber 4.9g
Sugars 1.9g
Protein 9.2g
Nutrition Facts
Servings: 4
Per Serving
Calories 340

Ingredients:

2 teaspoons olive oil

½ cup cooked black beans

2 tablespoons diced cheese

¼ cup chopped onion

½ teaspoon pepper

4 pastry sheets

Vegetable oil, to fry

Directions:

- Preheat a skillet over medium heat then pour olive oil into it.
- Once it is hot, stir in chopped onion then sautés until wilted and aromatic.
- Add the black beans into the skillet then season with pepper.
- Stirring occasionally and cook until the beans are completely seasoned and tender.
- Place the pastry sheets on a flat surface then drop about 2 tablespoons of the filling and diced cheese.
- Tightly roll the sheets until becoming logs.
- Pour vegetable oil in a saucepan over medium heat.
- Once it is hot, stir in the rolls then fry until lightly brown.
- Flip the rolls then continue frying until all of the roll's sides are lightly brown.
- Strain the oil then serves warm.

30 DAY PULSES CHALLENGE

Lentils Stew with Green Peas

Serving: 4

Nutrition Facts
Servings: 4
Per Serving
Calories 169
Total Fat 3.9g
Saturated Fat 0.6g
Trans Fat 0g
Cholesterol 0mg
Sodium 11mg
Potassium 393mg
Total Carb 24g
Dietary Fiber 11.7g
Sugars 1.6g
Protein 9.9g
Nutrition Facts
Servings: 4
Per Serving
Calories 169

Ingredients:

¾ cup uncooked lentils

¼ cup green peas

¼ cup chopped carrots

3 teaspoons olive oil

1 teaspoon minced garlic

1 bay leaf

2-¼ cups water

Directions:

30 DAY PULSES CHALLENGE

- Place lentils in a pot then pour water over the lentils. Bring to boil.
- Once it is boil, covers the pot with the lid then reduces the heat.
- Cook for about 30 minutes until the lentils are tender.
- Preheat a skillet over medium heat then pour olive oil into it.
- Once it is hot, stir in minced garlic then sautés until wilted and aromatic.
- Add green peas and chopped carrots into the skillet then sauté until wilted.
- Transfer the lentils to the skillet together with the liquid.
- Stirring occasionally and cook until the lentils are completely seasoned.
- Add bay leaf into the skillet and continue cooking until the gravy is thickened.
- Transfer to a serving dish then enjoy!

30 DAY PULSES CHALLENGE

Day 18

Breakfast : Sweet Soy Lentils Sushi
Lunch : Chickpeas and Fava Beans Fried Balls
Dinner : Healthy Beans Soup with Veggie

Sweet Soy Lentils Sushi

Serving: 4

Nutrition Facts
Servings: 4
Per Serving
Calories 242
Total Fat 7.5g
Saturated Fat 1.1g
Trans Fat 0g
Cholesterol 0mg
Sodium 233mg
Potassium 493mg
Total Carb 31.3g
Dietary Fiber 14.9g
Sugars 1.5g
Protein 13.4g
Nutrition Facts
Servings: 4
Per Serving
Calories 242

Ingredients:

2 tablespoons olive oil

1 cup uncooked lentils

¼ cup chopped onion

30 DAY PULSES CHALLENGE

1 tablespoon minced garlic

¼ teaspoon black pepper

1-tablespoon soy sauce

4 Nori sheets

2 tablespoons chopped leek

Directions:

- Wash and rinse the lentils then place in a pot with a lid.
- Pour water into a pot then bring to boil—3 cups of water for 1-cup lentils.
- Once it is boiled, stir in the lentils then cook for 20 minutes.
- Strain the cooked lentils then sets aside.
- Preheat a skillet over medium heat then pour olive oil into it.
- Once it is hot, stir in chopped onion and minced garlic then sautés until wilted and aromatic.
- Add the lentils into the skillet then season with black pepper and soy sauce.
- Stirring occasionally and cook until the lentils are completely seasoned and tender. Set aside.
- Place the nori sheets on a flat surface then drop the filling on top.
- Tightly roll the sheets until becoming logs.
- Using a very sharp knife cut the sushi into thick slices.
- Arrange on a serving dish then sprinkles chopped leek on top.
- Enjoy immediately.

30 DAY PULSES CHALLENGE

30 DAY PULSES CHALLENGE

Chickpeas and Fava Beans Fried Balls

Serving: 8

Nutrition Facts
Servings: 8
Per Serving
Calories 211
Total Fat 8.1g
Saturated Fat 1.1g
Trans Fat 0g
Cholesterol 0mg
Sodium 9mg
Potassium 425mg
Total Carb 26.6g
Dietary Fiber 9.2g
Sugars 3.9g
Protein 9.8g
Nutrition Facts
Servings: 8
Per Serving
Calories 211

Ingredients:

¼ cup olive oil

1 cup cooked chickpeas

1-cup fava beans

¼ cup chopped onion

1 teaspoon minced garlic

¼ teaspoon black pepper

Directions:
- Release the fava beans from the pod.

30 DAY PULSES CHALLENGE

- Pour water into a pot then bring to boil.
- Once it is boiled, stir in the fava beans then cook for a minutes.
- Strain the cooked fava beans then place in a food processor together with soaked chickpeas, chopped onion, minced garlic, and black pepper. Process until incorporated and smooth.
- Shape the mixture into small balls form then chill in the refrigerator for 10 minutes.
- Preheat a non-stick pan over medium heat then pour olive oil into it.
- Take the patties out from the refrigerator then place in the pan.
- Fry for about 3 minutes until brown then flips and cook for another 3 minutes until both sides of the fritters are brown.
- Once it is done, transfer to a serving dish. Enjoy!

30 DAY PULSES CHALLENGE

Healthy Beans Soup with Veggie

Serving: 4

Nutrition Facts
Servings: 4
Per Serving
Calories 174
Total Fat 1.9g
Saturated Fat 0.5g
Trans Fat 0g
Cholesterol 0mg
Sodium 769mg
Potassium 740mg
Total Carb 25.8g
Dietary Fiber 6.3g
Sugars 2.5g
Protein 13.8g
Nutrition Facts
Servings: 4
Per Serving
Calories 174

Ingredients:

- ¾ cup uncooked kidney beans
- ½ cup green peas
- 2 tablespoons sliced shallots
- ½ teaspoon pepper
- ¼ teaspoon nutmeg
- 4 cups vegetable broth

Directions:

30 DAY PULSES CHALLENGE

- Wash and rinse the kidney beans then place in a container with a lid.
- Pour water to cover the beans then covers the container with the lid and soaks the beans overnight—1-cup water for 3 cups beans.
- In the morning, rinse and strain the beans.
- Pour water into a pot then bring to boil.
- Once it is boiled, stir in the kidney beans then cook for an hour.
- Strain the cooked kidney beans then place in a pot.
- Add green peas into the pot then pour vegetable broth into the pot.
- Season with sliced shallot, pepper, and nutmeg then bring to boil.
- Once it is boiled, reduce the heat and cook for about 15 minutes.
- Transfer the soup to a bowl then serve warm.

30 DAY PULSES CHALLENGE

Day 19

Breakfast : Kidney Beans Thick Soup
Lunch : Lentils Coconut Burgers
Dinner : Garbanzo Beans with Green Kale

Kidney Beans Thick Soup

Serving: 4

Nutrition Facts
Servings: 4
Per Serving
Calories 244
Total Fat 7.8g
Saturated Fat 6.4g
Trans Fat 0g
Cholesterol 0mg
Sodium 10mg
Potassium 713mg
Total Carb 34.1g
Dietary Fiber 7.9g
Sugars 2g
Protein 11.4g
Nutrition Facts
Servings: 4
Per Serving
Calories 244

Ingredients:

1-cup cooked kidney beans

¼ cup chopped bacon

2 tablespoons rice flour

30 DAY PULSES CHALLENGE

½ cup coconut milk

½ teaspoon pepper

¼ teaspoon ginger

Directions:

- Wash and rinse the kidney beans then place in a bowl with a lid.
- Pour water to cover the beans then soak for at least 8 hours.
- After 8 hours, pour water into a pot then bring to boil.
- Once it is boiled, strain the beans then add into the hot water.
- Reduce the heat and bring to a simmer for about an hour.
- Take about ¼ cup of the beans liquid then combine with rice flour. Mix until incorporated.
- Return the liquid into the pot then stirring occasionally.
- Season with ginger and pepper then pour coconut milk into the pot.
- Bring to a simmer for about 4 minutes then transfers to a serving dish.
- Serve and enjoy warm.

30 DAY PULSES CHALLENGE

Lentils Coconut Burger

Serving: 4

Nutrition Facts
Servings: 4
Per Serving
Calories 269
Total Fat 10.9g
Saturated Fat 4g
Trans Fat 0g
Cholesterol 0mg
Sodium 5mg
Potassium 509mg
Total Carb 31.3g
Dietary Fiber 15.7g
Sugars 1.9g
Protein 12.9g
Nutrition Facts
Servings: 4
Per Serving
Calories 269

Ingredients:

- 2 tablespoons olive oil
- 1 cup uncooked lentils
- ½ cup grated coconut
- ¼ cup chopped onion
- 1 teaspoon minced garlic
- ¼ teaspoon black pepper

Directions:

- Wash and rinse the lentils then place in a pot with a lid.

- Pour water into a pot then bring to boil—3 cups of water for 1-cup lentils.
- Once it is boiled, stir in the lentils then cook for 20 minutes.
- Strain the cooked lentils then place in a food processor together with grated coconut, chopped onion, minced garlic, and black pepper. Process until incorporated and smooth.
- Shape the mixture into patties form then chill in the refrigerator for 10 minutes.
- Preheat a non-stick pan over medium heat then pour olive oil into it.
- Take the patties out from the refrigerator then place in the pan.
- Fry for about 3 minutes until brown then flips and cook for another 3 minutes until both sides of the patties are brown.
- Once it is done, transfer to a serving dish. Enjoy!

30 DAY PULSES CHALLENGE

Garbanzo Beans with Green Kale

Serving: 4

Nutrition Facts
Servings: 4
Per Serving
Calories 220
Total Fat 6.5g
Saturated Fat 0.8g
Trans Fat 0g
Cholesterol 0mg
Sodium 65mg
Potassium 485mg
Total Carb 32.2g
Dietary Fiber 8.9g
Sugars 5.5g
Protein 10g
Nutrition Facts
Servings: 4
Per Serving
Calories 220

Ingredients:

- 1-cup cooked Garbanzo beans
- 3 teaspoons olive oil
- 1 teaspoon sliced garlic
- 1 teaspoon sliced shallot
- 1 bay leaf
- ½ cup chopped kale
- ½ cup low sodium vegetable broth

Directions:

- Preheat a skillet over medium heat then pour olive oil into it.
- Once it is hot, stir in sliced garlic and shallot then sauté until wilted and aromatic.
- Add the cooked Garbanzo beans then stir in bay leaf.
- Stirring occasionally and cook until the beans are completely seasoned.
- After that, toss the chopped kale into the skillet then cook until wilted.
- Once it is boiled, reduce the heat and continue cooking until the gravy is thickened.
- Transfer to a serving dish then enjoy warm.

30 DAY PULSES CHALLENGE

Day 20

Breakfast : Spiced Green Peas
Lunch : Lentils Pasta with Goat Cheese
Dinner : Delicious Fava Beans with Browned Chicken

Spiced Green Peas

Serving: 4

Nutrition Facts
Servings: 2
Per Serving
Calories 193
Total Fat 5.7g
Saturated Fat 2.7g
Trans Fat 0g
Cholesterol 11mg
Sodium 14mg
Potassium 207mg
Total Carb 29.8g
Dietary Fiber 8.1g
Sugars 4.2g
Protein 7.2g
Nutrition Facts
Servings: 2
Per Serving
Calories 193

Ingredients:

1 cup cooked green peas

¼ cup ground millet

½ teaspoon ginger

30 DAY PULSES CHALLENGE

½ teaspoon chopped green chili

½ teaspoon cumin

2 teaspoons ghee

1-teaspoon pepper

Water

COMPLIMENTARY:

1 hard-boiled egg

Directions:

- Soak the millet for about ½ hour then sets aside.
- Place green peas, chili, and ginger in a food processor then processes until smooth and creamy.
- Preheat a pan over medium heat then add ghee and cumin into it.
- Stir in smooth green peas into the skillet then cook for about 5 minutes.
- Add soaked millet into the pan then pours water into it.
- Season with pepper then bring to a simmer for about 10 minutes.
- Transfer to a serving bowl then adds halved boiled eggs on top.
- Enjoy!

30 DAY PULSES CHALLENGE

Lentils Pasta with Goat Cheese

Serving: 5

Nutrition Facts
Servings: 5
Per Serving
Calories 246
Total Fat 6.6g
Saturated Fat 3.2g
Trans Fat 0g
Cholesterol 21mg
Sodium 48mg
Potassium 440mg
Total Carb 31.8g
Dietary Fiber 12g
Sugars 1.3g
Protein 15.1g
Nutrition Facts
Servings: 5
Per Serving
Calories 246

Ingredients:

- 1 cup cooked lentils
- ½ cup uncooked pasta
- ½ cup chopped kale
- 2 teaspoons olive oil
- 1 teaspoon minced garlic
- ¼ cup chopped onion
- ¼ teaspoon pepper
- 2 tablespoons goat cheese

Directions:

- Cook the pasta according to its direction. Set aside.
- Preheat a skillet over medium heat then pour olive oil into it.
- Once it is hot, stir in chopped onion and minced garlic then sauté until wilted and aromatic.
- Add the lentils and chopped kale into the skillet then dust pepper on top. Sauté until both lentils are completely seasoned and the kale are softened.
- Place the pasta on a serving dish then pour the lentils over the pasta.
- Sprinkle goat cheese on top then serves immediately.

Delicious Fava Beans with Browned Chicken

Serving: 4

Nutrition Facts
Servings: 4
Per Serving
Calories 175
Total Fat 4.4g
Saturated Fat 0.6g
Trans Fat 0.1g
Cholesterol 2mg
Sodium 556mg
Potassium 434mg
Total Carb 24g
Dietary Fiber 9.6g
Sugars 2.4g
Protein 11.3g
Nutrition Facts
Servings: 4
Per Serving
Calories 175

30 DAY PULSES CHALLENGE

Ingredients:

- 1 cup uncooked fava beans
- ¼ cup chicken chunks
- 2 teaspoons olive oil
- 1 teaspoon minced garlic
- 1 teaspoon sliced shallot
- 1 bay leaf
- ¼ cup low sodium soy sauce
- 1-cup water

Directions:

- Pour water in a pot then brings to boil.
- Meanwhile, take the bean pods then remove the seams.
- After that, open the pods then take the beans out.
- Place the beans in the hot water and let them sit for about 30 seconds.
- Strain the cooked fava beans then transfer to a bowl with cold water. This process will help you to automatically remove the coat of the beans.
- Preheat a skillet over medium heat then pour olive oil into it.
- Once it is hot, stir in minced garlic, sliced shallot, and bay leaf then sauté until wilted and aromatic.

30 DAY PULSES CHALLENGE

- Add chicken chunks into into the skillet then drizzle soy sauce over the chicken.
- Sauté until wilted then pour water into the skillet. Cook for a few minutes until the water is completely absorbed by the chicken.
- Stir in the fava beans then stir well.
- Transfer to a serving dish then enjoy!

30 DAY PULSES CHALLENGE

Day 21

Breakfast : Green Peas Casserole
Lunch : Scrumptious Indian Red Lentils
Dinner : Baked Beans with Pork

Green Peas Casserole

Serving: 4

Nutrition Facts
Servings: 4
Per Serving
Calories 218
Total Fat 16.8g
Saturated Fat 10.5g
Trans Fat 0g
Cholesterol 53mg
Sodium 151mg
Potassium 160mg
Total Carb 10.5g
Dietary Fiber 2.3g
Sugars 4.2g
Protein 7.3g
Nutrition Facts
Servings: 4
Per Serving
Calories 218

Ingredients:

1 cup green peas

2 tablespoons butter

1 teaspoon minced garlic

30 DAY PULSES CHALLENGE

1-tablespoon flour

¼ teaspoon pepper

½ cup fresh milk

4 tablespoons heavy cream

½ cup grated cheese

½ cup onion rings

Directions:

- Preheat an oven to 350 F then coat a casserole dish with cooking spray. Set aside.
- Pour water in a pot then bring to boil.
- Once it is boiled, place the green peas in the pot then cooks for 2 minutes until tender.
- Combine cooked green peas with butter, minced garlic, pepper, and cheese in a bowl.
- Pour fresh milk and heavy cream then mix until combined.
- Transfer the mixture to the prepared casserole dish then spread evenly.
- Sprinkle fried onion rings on the top then bake for about 20 minutes until set.
- Take the casserole out from the oven then serve warm.

30 DAY PULSES CHALLENGE

Scrumptious Indian red Lentils

Serving: 2

Nutrition Facts
Servings: 2
Per Serving
Calories 291
Total Fat 9.2g
Saturated Fat 1g
Trans Fat 0g
Cholesterol 0mg
Sodium 774mg
Potassium 779mg
Total Carb 34.3g
Dietary Fiber 15.8g
Sugars 2.4g
Protein 18g
Nutrition Facts
Servings: 2
Per Serving
Calories 291

Ingredients:

½ cup red lentils

1-½ tablespoons canola oil

3 teaspoons ginger

1 teaspoon minced garlic

¼ cup chopped scallions

1-½ teaspoons curry

2 tablespoons chopped carrots

2 cups vegetable broth

Directions:

30 DAY PULSES CHALLENGE

- Preheat a skillet over medium heat then pour canola oil into it.
- Once it is hot, stir in minced garlic then sautés until wilted and aromatic.
- Add scallions, ginger, and curry into the skillet then stir well.
- After that, stir in the red lentils and chopped carrot then pour vegetable broth into the skillet. Bring to boil.
- Once it is boiled, reduce the heat and cook for about 20 minutes until the lentils are tender.
- Transfer to a serving dish then enjoy!

30 DAY PULSES CHALLENGE

Baked Beans with Pork

Serving: 4

Nutrition Facts
Servings: 5
Per Serving
Calories 283
Total Fat 2g
Saturated Fat 0.7g
Trans Fat 0g
Cholesterol 33mg
Sodium 136mg
Potassium 979mg
Total Carb 46.5g
Dietary Fiber 6.3g
Sugars 22.4g
Protein 21.6g
Nutrition Facts
Servings: 5
Per Serving
Calories 283

Ingredients:

1 cup uncooked white beans

¼ cup chopped onion

½ lb. chopped pork

¼ cup raw honey

3 tablespoons brown sugar

3 tablespoons ketchup

3 teaspoons lemon juice

Directions:

- Wash and rinse the white beans then place in a bowl with a lid.
- Pour water to cover the white beans then soak for at least 8 hours.
- After 8 hours, pour water into a pot then bring to boil.
- Once it is boiled, strain the white beans then add into the hot water.
- Reduce the heat and bring to a simmer for about an hour.
- Strain the cooked white beans then set aside.
- Preheat an oven to 350 F.
- Next, place all of the ingredients in a baking dish then stir well.
- Bake for about 45 minutes then remove from the oven.
- Transfer to a serving dish then enjoy!

30 DAY PULSES CHALLENGE

Day 22

Breakfast : Soft Waffle with Green Peas
Lunch : White Beans Tomato Pasta
Dinner : Warm Lentils Soup with Spinach

Soft Waffle with Green Peas

Serving: 4

Nutrition Facts
Servings: 4
Per Serving
Calories 284
Total Fat 15.4g
Saturated Fat 13.3g
Trans Fat 0g
Cholesterol 3mg
Sodium 20mg
Potassium 259mg
Total Carb 33.5g
Dietary Fiber 3.2g
Sugars 12.9g
Protein 4.7g
Nutrition Facts
Servings: 4
Per Serving
Calories 284

Ingredients:

1 cup cooked green peas

1-cup multi purpose flour

3 teaspoons palm sugar

30 DAY PULSES CHALLENGE

1-teaspoon baking powder

1 cup almond milk

2 tablespoons olive oil

1 organic egg

Directions:

- Place green peas in a blender together then add flour, pal sugar, and baking powder.
- Pour almond milk and olive oil then add egg into the blender. Blend until smooth and incorporated.
- Preheat a waffle maker then make the waffles according to the directions.
- Arrange the waffles on a serving dish
- Serve and enjoy!

30 DAY PULSES CHALLENGE

White Beans Tomato Macaroni

Serving: 4

Nutrition Facts
Servings: 4
Per Serving
Calories 241
Total Fat 3g
Saturated Fat 0.5g
Trans Fat 0g
Cholesterol 0mg
Sodium 105mg
Potassium 1093mg
Total Carb 41.5g
Dietary Fiber 8.6g
Sugars 3.4g
Protein 13.8g
Nutrition Facts
Servings 4
Per Serving
Calories 241

Ingredients:

1 cup cooked white beans

3 cups water

2 teaspoons olive oil

½ cup unsweetened tomato juice

2 tablespoons tomato paste

1 teaspoon minced garlic

½ teaspoon pepper

1 tablespoon chopped celery

½ cup uncooked macaroni

30 DAY PULSES CHALLENGE

Directions:

- Cook the macaroni according to the package direction then sets aside.
- Preheat a skillet over medium heat then pour olive oil into it.
- Once it is hot, stir in minced garlic then sautés until wilted and aromatic.
- Add tomato paste and the cooked white beans then pour tomato juice into the skillet.
- Season with pepper, then sauté until the white beans are completely seasoned.
- At last, stir in the cooked macaroni and chopped celery then mix well.
- Transfer to a serving dish then enjoy immediately.

30 DAY PULSES CHALLENGE

Warm Lentils Soup with Spinach

Serving: 4

Nutrition Facts
Servings: 4
Per Serving
Calories 171
Total Fat 1.8g
Saturated Fat 0.5g
Trans Fat 0g
Cholesterol 0mg
Sodium 770mg
Potassium 583mg
Total Carb 23.7g
Dietary Fiber 11.3g
Sugars 1.9g
Protein 14.3g
Nutrition Facts
Servings: 4
Per Serving
Calories 171

Ingredients:

- ¾ cup uncooked lentils
- ¼ cup chopped spinach
- 2 tablespoons diced carrots
- 2 tablespoons sliced onion
- ½ teaspoon pepper
- ¼ teaspoon nutmeg
- 4 cups vegetable broth

Directions:

- Wash and rinse the lentils then place in a pot with a lid.
- Pour water into a pot then bring to boil—3 cups of water for 1-cup lentils.
- Once it is boiled, stir in the lentils then cook for 20 minutes.
- Strain the cooked lentils then place in a pot.
- Add diced carrots into the pot then pour vegetable broth into the pot.
- Season with sliced onion, pepper, and nutmeg then bring to boil.
- Once it is boiled, reduce the heat and cook for about 15 minutes.
- Add the chopped spinach into the pot then stir vigorously—the heat remained in the soup will make the spinach wilted.
- Transfer the soup to a bowl then serve warm.

30 DAY PULSES CHALLENGE

Day 23

Breakfast : Soft Beans Patties
Lunch : Spicy Lentils Noodle
Dinner : Red Hot Green Peas

Soft Beans Patties

Serving: 4

Nutrition Facts
Servings: 4
Per Serving
Calories 259
Total Fat 8.9g
Saturated Fat 1.5g
Trans Fat 0g
Cholesterol 41mg
Sodium 76mg
Potassium 659mg
Total Carb 33.4g
Dietary Fiber 7.3g
Sugars 1.5g
Protein 12.7g
Nutrition Facts
Servings: 4
Per Serving
Calories 259

Ingredients:

1 cup cooked kidney beans

3 cups water

¼ cup breadcrumbs

30 DAY PULSES CHALLENGE

1 organic egg

1 teaspoon minced garlic

¼ teaspoon pepper

2 tablespoons olive oil

Directions:

- Place the kidney beans in a food processor together with breadcrumbs and egg then season with minced garlic and pepper. Process until smooth.
- Shape the mixture into small patties form-- don't make it to big.
- Preheat a non-stick pan over medium heat then pour olive oil into it.
- Once the oil is hot, place the chickpeas patties on the non-stick pan.
- Fry for about 3 minutes until brown then flips and cook for another 3 minutes until both sides of the fritters are brown.
- Once it is done, transfer to a serving dish. Enjoy!

30 DAY PULSES CHALLENGE

Spicy Lentils Noodles

Serving: 4

Nutrition Facts
Servings: 4
Per Serving
Calories 244
Total Fat 5.1g
Saturated Fat 0.8g
Trans Fat 0g
Cholesterol 16mg
Sodium 3936mg
Potassium 387mg
Total Carb 37.6g
Dietary Fiber 11.8g
Sugars 1.8g
Protein 12.4g
Nutrition Facts
Servings 4
Per Serving
Calories 244

Ingredients:

- ¾ cup uncooked lentils
- 2 tablespoons red chili flakes
- 3 teaspoons olive oil
- 1 teaspoon minced garlic
- 1 bay leaf
- 2 tablespoons soy sauce
- 1-teaspoon brown sugar
- ½ lb. uncooked noodles

Directions:

- Place lentils in a pot then pour water over the lentils. Bring to boil.
- Once it is boil, covers the pot with the lid then reduces the heat.
- Cook for about 30 minutes until the lentils are tender.
- Preheat a skillet over medium heat then pour olive oil into it.
- Once it is hot, stir in minced garlic and red chili flakes then sautés until wilted and aromatic.
- Add lentils into the skillet together with liquid then stir occasionally.
- Add bay leaf, soy sauce, and brown sugar into the skillet.
- Continue cooking until the gravy is thickened.
- Cook the noodles according to the directions then place on a serving platter.
- Pour the cooked lentils over the noodle then serve immediately.

30 DAY PULSES CHALLENGE

Red Hot Green Peas

Serving: 4

Nutrition Facts
Servings: 2
Per Serving
Calories 122
Total Fat 3.2g
Saturated Fat 0.5g
Trans Fat 0g
Cholesterol 0mg
Sodium 16mg
Potassium 412mg
Total Carb 19.8g
Dietary Fiber 6.7g
Sugars 8.3g
Protein 5.4g
Nutrition Facts
Servings: 2
Per Serving
Calories 122

Ingredients:

- 1 cup green peas
- ½ cup chopped red chili
- 1 tablespoon minced shallot
- 1 tablespoon minced garlic
- 1 bay leaf
- 1-teaspoon olive oil
- ½ cup water
- 2 tablespoons chopped tomato

Directions:

- Pour water in a pot then bring to boil.
- Once it is boiled, place the green peas in the pot then cooks for 2 minutes until tender. Set aside.
- Place red chili in a food processor together with shallot, garlic, and tomato. Process until smooth and incorporated.
- Preheat a skillet over medium heat then pour olive oil into it.
- Once it is hot, stir in the spices mixture then sauté until aromatic.
- Next, add green peas into the skillet then stir the peas are completely seasoned.
- Pour water into the skillet then bring to boil.
- Once it is boiled, reduce the heat and cook until the gravy is thickened.
- Transfer to a serving dish then enjoy with a bowl of rice. Enjoy!

30 DAY PULSES CHALLENGE

Day 24

Breakfast : Lentils Scrambled Egg
Lunch : Beans and Shrimps in Tomato Pond
Dinner : Green Peas in Mixed Vegetable

Scrambled Lentils Veggie

Serving: 8

Nutrition Facts
Servings: 8
Per Serving
Calories 216
Total Fat 4.2g
Saturated Fat 1.7g
Trans Fat 0g
Cholesterol 86mg
Sodium 45mg
Potassium 494mg
Total Carb 29.5g
Dietary Fiber 14.7g
Sugars 1.3g
Protein 15.2g
Nutrition Facts
Servings: 8
Per Serving
Calories 216

Ingredients:

2 cups uncooked lentils

4 organic eggs

1-tablespoon butter

30 DAY PULSES CHALLENGE

¼ teaspoon pepper

¼ cup chopped leek

Directions:

- Place lentils in a pot then pour water over the lentils. Bring to boil.
- Once it is boil, covers the pot with the lid then reduces the heat.
- Cook for about 30 minutes until the lentils are tender.
- Strain the lentils then sets aside.
- Crack the eggs then place in a bowl. Using a whisker whisk the eggs until completely beaten. Set aside.
- Preheat anon-stick pan over medium heat then place butter into it.
- Once the butter is melted, pour the egg into the pan then scramble quickly.
- When the egg is set, stir in lentils and chopped leek then sauté until well combined.
- Transfer to a serving dish then enjoy!

30 DAY PULSES CHALLENGE

Beans and Shrimps in Tomato Pond

Serving: 4

Nutrition Facts
Servings: 4
Per Serving
Calories 148
Total Fat 4g
Saturated Fat 0.8g
Trans Fat 0g
Cholesterol 179mg
Sodium 219mg
Potassium 425mg
Total Carb 7.2g
Dietary Fiber 2.1g
Sugars 2.8g
Protein 20.7g
Nutrition Facts
Servings: 4
Per Serving
Calories 148

Ingredients:

- 1 cup cooked beans
- 3 cups water
- ¼ cup fresh shrimps
- 2 teaspoons olive oil
- 2 large tomatoes
- 1 teaspoon minced garlic
- ½ teaspoon pepper

Directions:

30 DAY PULSES CHALLENGE

- Place the tomatoes in a steamer then steam until soft.
- Press the steamed tomato and strain the liquid. Set aside.
- Preheat a skillet over medium heat then pour olive oil into it.
- Once it is hot, stir in minced garlic then sautés until wilted and aromatic.
- Add shrimps into the skillet then sauté until the color of the shrimps change into pink.
- Season with pepper then stir in the beans.
- Pour the tomato liquid and stir occasionally.
- Transfer to to serving bowl then enjoy immediately.

Green Peas in Mixed Vegetables

Serving: 4

Nutrition Facts
Servings: 2
Per Serving
Calories 163
Total Fat 3.3g
Saturated Fat 0.9g
Trans Fat 0g
Cholesterol 0mg
Sodium 1549mg
Potassium 775mg
Total Carb 18.3g
Dietary Fiber 5.3g
Sugars 6.8g
Protein 15g
Nutrition Facts
Servings: 2
Per Serving
Calories 163

30 DAY PULSES CHALLENGE

Ingredients:

- 1 cup cooked green peas
- ¼ cup chopped carrots
- ¼ cup chopped green beans
- ½ cup broccoli florets
- 2 tablespoons sliced shallots
- ½ teaspoon pepper
- ¼ teaspoon nutmeg
- 4 cups vegetable broth

Directions:

- Place all of the ingredients in a pot then bring to boil.
- Once it is boiled, reduce the heat then continue cooking for about 5 minutes.
- Once it is done, remove from the heat then transfer to a serving bowl.
- Serve and enjoy warm.

30 DAY PULSES CHALLENGE

Day 25

Breakfast : Creamy Mung Beans Milk Porridge
Lunch : Delicious Lentils Salmon
Dinner : Hot Beans Rice

Creamy Mung Beans Milk Porridge

Serving: 4

Nutrition Facts
Servings: 4
Per Serving
Calories 242
Total Fat 1.9g
Saturated Fat 0.9g
Trans Fat 0g
Cholesterol 5mg
Sodium 42mg
Potassium 687mg
Total Carb 44.1g
Dietary Fiber 8.5g
Sugars 14.8g
Protein 14.4g
Nutrition Facts
Servings: 4
Per Serving
Calories 242

Ingredients:

1 cup uncooked Mung beans

3 cups water

1-cup fresh milk

2 tablespoons honey

Directions:

- Wash and rinse the Mung beans then place in a bowl with a lid.
- Pour water to cover the beans then soak for at least 8 hours.
- After 8 hours, pour 3 cups water into a pot then bring to boil.
- Once it is boiled, strain the Mung beans then add into the hot water.
- Reduce the heat and bring to a simmer for about an hour.
- Pour fresh milk over the beans then remove from heat.
- Using an immersion blender, blend the porridge until smooth.
- Transfer the creamy porridge to a serving bowl then drizzles honey on top. Stir well.
- Serve and enjoy warm.

30 DAY PULSES CHALLENGE

Delicious Lentils Salmon

Serving: 5

Nutrition Facts
Servings: 5
Per Serving
Calories 311
Total Fat 11.7g
Saturated Fat 1.7g
Trans Fat 0g
Cholesterol 40mg
Sodium 69mg
Potassium 754mg
Total Carb 24.6g
Dietary Fiber 12.1g
Sugars 1.4g
Protein 27.8g
Nutrition Facts
Servings: 5
Per Serving
Calories 311

Ingredients:

1-cup lentils

½ teaspoon black pepper

2 tablespoons olive oil

1 lb. salmon fillet

¼ cup diced carrots

¼ cup diced cucumber

2 teaspoons Dijon mustard

¼ cup chopped onion

Directions:

- Wash and rinse the lentils then place in a pot with a lid.
- Pour water into a pot then bring to boil—3 cups of water for 1-cup lentils.
- Once it is boiled, stir in the lentils then cook for 20 minutes.
- Strain the cooked lentils then set aside.
- Preheat a non-stick pan over medium heat then brush with olive oil.
- Once it is hot, place the salmon on the pan then sprinkle black pepper over the salmon.
- Cook for about 5 minutes then flip the salmon.
- Continue cooking until the salmon is opaque. Remove from heat then set aside.
- Preheat a skillet over medium heat then pour the remaining olive oil into it.
- Once it is hot, stir in chopped onion and then sautés until wilted and aromatic.
- Add carrots, cucumber, and lentils into the skillet then seasons with Dijon mustard.
- Cook for about 2 minutes then remove from heat.
- Transfer the lentils and vegetables to a serving platter then place the salmon on top.
- Serve and enjoy warm.

30 DAY PULSES CHALLENGE

Hot Beans Rice

Serving: 5

Nutrition Facts
Servings: 4
Per Serving
Calories 226
Total Fat 4.2g
Saturated Fat 0.6g
Trans Fat 0g
Cholesterol 0mg
Sodium 87mg
Potassium 762mg
Total Carb 36.6g
Dietary Fiber 8.1g
Sugars 1.4g
Protein 11.6g
Nutrition Facts
Servings: 4
Per Serving
Calories 226

Ingredients:

1 cup uncooked Pinto beans

2 tablespoons diced carrot

1 tablespoon red chili flakes

1 teaspoon chopped celery

1-tablespoon olive oil

½ cup minced garlic

1-teaspoon pepper

1-teaspoon soy sauce

Directions:

- Wash and rinse the kidney beans then place in a container with a lid.
- Pour water to cover the beans then covers the container with the lid and soaks the beans overnight—1-cup water for 3 cups beans.
- In the morning, rinse and strain the beans.
- Pour water into a pot then bring to boil.
- Once it is boiled, stir in the kidney beans then cook for an hour.
- Strain the cooked kidney beans then place in a food processor. Process until becoming crumbled.
- Preheat a skillet over medium heat then pour olive oil into it.
- Once it is hot, stir in minced garlic and then sautés until wilted and aromatic.
- Add beans crumbles into the skillet then dust pepper on top.
- Drizzle soy sauce over the beans crumbled then mixes well.
- Stir in red chili flakes and chopped celery then using a wooden spatula, mix them all.
- Cook for about 2 minutes then transfer to a serving dish.
- Serve and enjoy warm.

30 DAY PULSES CHALLENGE

Day 26

Breakfast : Chickpeas Honey Salads
Lunch : Cheesy Bean Lasagna
Dinner : Spicy Black Beans Turkey

Chickpeas Honey Salads

Serving: 4

Nutrition Facts
Servings: 4
Per Serving
Calories 247
Total Fat 3g
Saturated Fat 0.3g
Trans Fat 0g
Cholesterol 0mg
Sodium 20mg
Potassium 464mg
Total Carb 48g
Dietary Fiber 8.8g
Sugars 22.9g
Protein 9.8g
Nutrition Facts
Servings: 4
Per Serving
Calories 247

Ingredients:

1-½ cups dried chickpeas

4-½ cups water

2 tablespoons diced tomato

30 DAY PULSES CHALLENGE

¼ cup raw honey

Any green for garnish

Directions:

- Wash and rinse the chickpeas then place in a bowl with a lid.
- Pour water to cover the chickpeas then soak overnight.
- In the morning, pour water into a pot then bring to boil.
- Once it is boiled, strain the chickpeas then add into the hot water.
- Reduce the heat and bring to a simmer for about an hour.
- Strain the cooked chickpeas then place in a salad bowl.
- Pour honey over the chickpeas then mix well.
- Serve and enjoy!

30 DAY PULSES CHALLENGE

Cheesy Bean Lasagna

Serving: 4

Nutrition Facts
Servings: 4
Per Serving
Calories 202
Total Fat 3.2g
Saturated Fat 0.5g
Trans Fat 0g
Cholesterol 1mg
Sodium 563mg
Potassium 779mg
Total Carb 32.8g
Dietary Fiber 7.8g
Sugars 1.5g
Protein 11.9g
Nutrition Facts
Servings: 4
Per Serving
Calories 202

Ingredients:

1 cup cooked beans

1-tablespoon taco seasoning

½ cup softened cream cheese

1 cup chopped green chili

1-cup salsa

2 cup chopped lettuce

¼ cup tomato sauce

2 cups grated cheese

½ cup olive

30 DAY PULSES CHALLENGE

Directions:

- Combine beans with taco seasoning then mix until combined. Set aside.
- Combine softened cream cheese with green chili then also mix well. Set aside.
- Preheat an oven to 350 F then coat a casserole dish with cooking spray.
- Place the beans on the bottom of the prepared casserole dish then spread evenly.
- Layer with cream cheese mixture, lettuce, salsa, tomato sauce, and grated cheese.
- Sprinkle olive on top then bake for about 10 minutes until the cheese is lightly brown.
- Remove from the oven then serve warm.

30 DAY PULSES CHALLENGE

Spicy Black Beans Turkey

Serving: 4

Nutrition Facts
Servings: 4
Per Serving
Calories 202
Total Fat 3.2g
Saturated Fat 0.5g
Trans Fat 0g
Cholesterol 1mg
Sodium 563mg
Potassium 779mg
Total Carb 32.8g
Dietary Fiber 7.8g
Sugars 1.5g
Protein 11.9g
Nutrition Facts
Servings: 4
Per Serving
Calories 202

Ingredients:

1 cup cooked black beans

¼ lb. turkey breast

2 teaspoons olive oil

1 teaspoon minced garlic

1 teaspoon sliced shallot

1-teaspoon red pepper flakes

1 bay leaf

¼ cup low sodium soy sauce

1-teaspoon pepper

1-cup water

Directions:

- Place the chicken breast in a pot then pour water to cover. Bring to boil.
- Once it is boiled, reduce the heat and cook until the turkey is tender.
- Next, take the turkey out from the pot and let it sit until cold.
- After that, cut the cooked turkey into chunks then sets aside.
- Preheat a skillet over medium heat then pour olive oil into it.
- Once it is hot, stir in minced garlic, sliced shallot, red pepper flakes, and bay leaf then sauté until wilted and aromatic.
- Add the cooked turkey into the skillet then drizzles soy sauce over the chicken.
- Stir in the black beans then stir well.
- Season with pepper then sauté until all of the ingredients are completely seasoned.
- Transfer to a serving dish then enjoy!

30 DAY PULSES CHALLENGE

Day 27

Breakfast : Healthy Colorful Salads
Lunch : Mixed Beans and Peas Pasta
Dinner : Smooth Green Peas Soup

Healthy Colorful Salads

Serving: 4

Nutrition Facts
Servings: 4
Per Serving
Calories 204
Total Fat 4.1g
Saturated Fat 0.6g
Trans Fat 0g
Cholesterol 0mg
Sodium 8mg
Potassium 768mg
Total Carb 32.7g
Dietary Fiber 7.5g
Sugars 3.6g
Protein 11g
Nutrition Facts
Servings: 4
Per Serving
Calories 204

Ingredients:

1 cup cooked red beans

1 medium cucumber

1 medium radish

30 DAY PULSES CHALLENGE

¼ cup pomegranate

1 tablespoon lemon juice

1-tablespoon olive oil

Directions:

- Cut the cucumber and radish into slices.
- Place the sliced cucumber and radish in a salad bowl then add the remaining ingredients.
- Using two forks mix all the ingredients until combined.
- Serve and enjoy immediately.

30 DAY PULSES CHALLENGE

Mixed Beans and Peas Salads

Serving: 3

Nutrition Facts
Servings: 4
Per Serving
Calories 267
Total Fat 2.4g
Saturated Fat 0.4g
Trans Fat 0g
Cholesterol 12mg
Sodium 30mg
Potassium 1001mg
Total Carb 48.2g
Dietary Fiber 10.3g
Sugars 6.3g
Protein 15.5g
Nutrition Facts
Servings: 4
Per Serving
Calories 267

Ingredients:

1 cup cooked green peas

1 cup cooked kidney beans

½ cup chopped green beans

½ cup chopped red peppers

½ cup uncooked pasta

¼ cup tomato paste

1 tablespoon chopped onion

1-teaspoon olive oil

Directions:

30 DAY PULSES CHALLENGE

- Cook the pasta according to its direction. Set aside.
- Preheat a skillet then pour olive oil into it.
- Once it is hot, stir in chopped onion then sautés until aromatic.
- Add tomato paste into the skillet then bring to a simmer.
- After that, stir in green peas, kidney beans, and pasta into the skillet then mix well.
- Transfer to a serving dish then enjoy!

Smooth Green Peas Soup

Serving: 4

Nutrition Facts
Servings: 2
Per Serving
Calories 144
Total Fat 4.9g
Saturated Fat 0.7g
Trans Fat 0g
Cholesterol 0mg
Sodium 231mg
Potassium 300mg
Total Carb 19.7g
Dietary Fiber 4.8g
Sugars 8.3g
Protein 6.4g
Nutrition Facts
Servings: 2
Per Serving
Calories 144

Ingredients:

1-cup fresh green peas

1 ½ teaspoons olive oil

30 DAY PULSES CHALLENGE

½ cup chopped onion

1 teaspoon minced garlic

1-cup low sodium vegetable broth

¼ teaspoon pepper

½ cup soymilk

Directions:

- Place the green peas in a steamer then steam until tender. Set aside.
- Preheat olive oil in a pot over medium heat.
- Stir in chopped onion and minced garlic then sauté until wilted and aromatic.
- Next, stir in lentils together with mashed potato and grated carrot then pour vegetable broth into the pot. Bring to boil.
- Once it is boil, season with pepper then cover the pot with the lid. Reduce the heat.
- Cook for about 30 minutes until the lentils are tender.
- After that, open the lid then pour soymilk over the soup. Bring to a simmer.
- Once it is done, remove from the heat and let it warm.
- Using an immersion blender, blend the soup until smooth.
- Transfer to a soup bowl and enjoy warm.

Day 28

Breakfast : Nourishing Beans and Shrimps
Lunch : Chickpeas Bites with Curry Spices
Dinner : Kidney Beans Stew

Nourishing Beans and Shrimps

Serving: 2

Nutrition Facts
Servings: 2
Per Serving
Calories 211
Total Fat 12.5g
Saturated Fat 7.6g
Trans Fat 0g
Cholesterol 120mg
Sodium 189mg
Potassium 252mg
Total Carb 11.1g
Dietary Fiber 3.7g
Sugars 4.1g
Protein 13.7g
Nutrition Facts
Servings: 2
Per Serving
Calories 211

Ingredients:

1 cup uncooked green peas

½ cup shrimps

2 tablespoons butter

30 DAY PULSES CHALLENGE

Directions:

- Pour water in a pot then bring to boil.
- Once it is boiled, place the green peas in the pot then cooks for 2 minutes until tender. Set aside.
- Preheat a saucepan over medium heat then place butter into it.
- Once it is melted, stir in the shrimps and sautés until the shrimps are pink.
- Add green peas into the saucepan and stir well.
- Transfer to a serving dish then enjoy immediately.

30 DAY PULSES CHALLENGE

Chickpeas Bites with Curry Spices

Serving: 4

Nutrition Facts
Servings: 4
Per Serving
Calories 250
Total Fat 10.1g
Saturated Fat 1.3g
Trans Fat 0g
Cholesterol 0mg
Sodium 13mg
Potassium 467mg
Total Carb 32g
Dietary Fiber 9.1g
Sugars 5.8g
Protein 9.9g
Nutrition Facts
Servings: 4
Per Serving
Calories 250

Ingredients:

- 2 tablespoons olive oil
- 1 cup uncooked chickpeas
- ¼ cup chopped onion
- 1 teaspoon minced garlic
- 1-teaspoon curry
- ¼ teaspoon turmeric
- 2 tablespoons chopped leek

Directions:

- Place the chickpeas then place in a container with a lid. Make sure that you have washed and rinsed them before.
- Pour water to cover the chickpeas then covers the container with the lid and soaks the chickpeas overnight.
- Place the soaked chickpeas in a food processor together with chopped onion, chopped parsley, minced garlic, curry powder, and turmeric. Process until smooth and becoming dough.
- Shape the mixture into small patties form-- don't make it to big.
- Preheat a non-stick pan over medium heat then pour olive oil into it.
- Once the oil is hot, place the chickpeas patties on the non-stick pan.
- Fry for about 3 minutes until brown then flips and cook for another 3 minutes until both sides of the fritters are brown.
- Once it is done, transfer to a serving dish. Enjoy!

30 DAY PULSES CHALLENGE

Kidney Beans Stew

Serving: 4

Nutrition Facts
Servings: 4
Per Serving
Calories 164
Total Fat 4.4g
Saturated Fat 0.6g
Trans Fat 0g
Cholesterol 0mg
Sodium 11mg
Potassium 595mg
Total Carb 24.5g
Dietary Fiber 6.1g
Sugars 2.2g
Protein 8.5g
Nutrition Facts
Servings: 4
Per Serving
Calories 164

Ingredients:

¾ cup cooked kidney beans

3 teaspoons olive oil

½ teaspoon ginger

1 teaspoon minced garlic

3 teaspoons cumin

½ teaspoon rosemary

1 ½ teaspoons garam masala

1 bay leave

½ teaspoon oregano

1 ½ teaspoons tamarind

30 DAY PULSES CHALLENGE

½ cup water

Directions:

- Preheat a skillet over medium heat then pour olive oil into it.
- Once it is hot, stir in minced garlic then sautés until wilted and aromatic.
- Add the cooked kidney beans then seasons with ginger, cumin, rosemary, garam masala, bay leaf, oregano, and tamarind.
- Stirring occasionally and cook until the beans are completely seasoned.
- Pour water into the skillet then bring to boil.
- Once it is boiled, reduce the heat and continue cooking until the gravy is thickened.
- Transfer to a serving dish then enjoy with warm rice.

30 DAY PULSES CHALLENGE

Day 29

Breakfast : Cheesy Lentils Tender
Lunch : Savory Lentils Rolls
Dinner : Chickpeas in Tomato Gravy

Cheesy Lentils Tender

Serving: 4

Nutrition Facts
Servings: 4
Per Serving
Calories 229
Total Fat 6.9g
Saturated Fat 4.1g
Trans Fat 0g
Cholesterol 17mg
Sodium 57mg
Potassium 473mg
Total Carb 29.2g
Dietary Fiber 14.7g
Sugars 1.2g
Protein 12.9g
Nutrition Facts
Servings: 4
Per Serving
Calories 229

Ingredients:
- 1 cup uncooked lentils
- 2 tablespoons chopped carrots
- 1 tablespoon grated cheese

30 DAY PULSES CHALLENGE

2 tablespoons butter

Directions:

- Wash and rinse the lentils then place in a pot with a lid.
- Pour water into a pot then bring to boil—3 cups of water for 1-cup lentils.
- Once it is boiled, stir in the lentils then cook for 20 minutes.
- Strain the cooked lentils then set aside.
- Preheat a saucepan over medium heat then place butter into it.
- Once it is melted, stir in the lentils and carrot then sautés until the lentils and carrot are completely coated with butter.
- Transfer to a serving dish then sprinkle grated cheese on top.
- Serve and enjoy immediately.

30 DAY PULSES CHALLENGE

Savory Lentils Rolls

Serving: 5

Nutrition Facts
Servings: 5
Per Serving
Calories 256
Total Fat 8.4g
Saturated Fat 1.5g
Trans Fat 0g
Cholesterol 65mg
Sodium 107mg
Potassium 428mg
Total Carb 32.2g
Dietary Fiber 12.4g
Sugars 1.9g
Protein 13.7g
Nutrition Facts
Servings: 5
Per Serving
Calories 256

Ingredients:

2 tablespoons olive oil

1 cup cooked lentils

½ cup whole-wheat breadcrumbs

2 organic eggs

¼ cup chopped onion

1 tablespoon minced garlic

¼ teaspoon black pepper

Directions:

30 DAY PULSES CHALLENGE

- Place the cooked lentils in a food processor together with whole-wheat breadcrumbs, chopped onion, eggs, minced garlic, and black pepper. Process until incorporated and smooth.
- Shape the mixture into log form then wrap with aluminum foil.
- Preheat a steamer then steam the roll for about 15 minutes until set.
- Once it is set, take it out from the steamer and let it cool for a few minutes.
- When the roll is cool, unwrap the roll then place on a non-stick pan.
- Brush with olive oil then bakes over medium heat.
- Place the roll on a serving dish then cut into slices.
- Serve and enjoy!

30 DAY PULSES CHALLENGE

Chickpeas in Tomato Gravy

Serving: 4

Nutrition Facts
Servings: 4
Per Serving
Calories 215
Total Fat 5.5g
Saturated Fat 0.7g
Trans Fat 0g
Cholesterol 0mg
Sodium 27mg
Potassium 584mg
Total Carb 33.4g
Dietary Fiber 9.5g
Sugars 7g
Protein 10.3g
Nutrition Facts
Servings: 4
Per Serving
Calories 215

Ingredients:

1 cup dried chickpeas

3 cups water

2 teaspoons olive oil

½ cup chopped tomato

2 tablespoons tomato paste

1 teaspoon minced garlic

½ teaspoon pepper

1-tablespoon lemon

Directions:

30 DAY PULSES CHALLENGE

- Wash and rinse the chickpeas then place in a bowl with a lid.
- Pour water to cover the chickpeas then soak overnight.
- In the morning, pour water into a pot then bring to boil.
- Once it is boiled, strain the chickpeas then add into the hot water.
- Reduce the heat and bring to a simmer for about an hour.
- Strain the cooked chickpeas then set aside.
- Preheat a skillet over medium heat then pour olive oil into it.
- Once it is hot, stir in minced garlic then sautés until wilted and aromatic.
- Add tomato paste chopped tomato, and chickpeas.
- Season with pepper and lemon juice then sauté until the chickpeas are completely seasoned.
- Pour the liquid and stir occasionally.
- Transfer the cooked chickpeas to serving bowl then sprinkles chopped celery.
- Serve and enjoy!

30 DAY PULSES CHALLENGE

Day 30

Breakfast : Green Peas Pancake
Lunch : Beans Avocado Salads
Dinner : Lentils Balls Tomato Soup

Green Peas Pancake

Serving: 4

Nutrition Facts
Servings: 4
Per Serving
Calories 284
Total Fat 15.4g
Saturated Fat 13.3g
Trans Fat 0g
Cholesterol 3mg
Sodium 20mg
Potassium 259mg
Total Carb 33.5g
Dietary Fiber 3.2g
Sugars 12.9g
Protein 4.7g
Nutrition Facts
Servings: 4
Per Serving
Calories 284

Ingredients:

1 cup cooked green peas

1 cup almond milk

½ cup multi purpose flour

30 DAY PULSES CHALLENGE

¼ cup brown sugar

1-teaspoon butter

Directions:

- Place green peas in a blender together with flour and brown sugar.
- Pour almond milk into the blender then blend until smooth and incorporated.
- Transfer to bowl then prepare the pan.
- Preheat a non-stick frying pan over medium heat.
- Once it is hot, grease with butter then pour about ¼ cup of mixture into the pan.
- Cook the pancake for about 2 minutes then flips it.
- Cook for another 2 minutes until both sides of the pancakes are lightly golden.
- Transfer to a serving plate then repeats with the remaining mixture.
- Serve and enjoy immediately.

30 DAY PULSES CHALLENGE

Beans Avocado Salads

Serving: 4

Nutrition Facts
Servings: 4
Per Serving
Calories 129
Total Fat 2.1g
Saturated Fat 0.4g
Trans Fat 0g
Cholesterol 0mg
Sodium 4mg
Potassium 367mg
Total Carb 23.6g
Dietary Fiber 4.2g
Sugars 9.2g
Protein 5.4g
Nutrition Facts
Servings: 4
Per Serving
Calories 129

Ingredients:

- ½ cup uncooked kidney beans
- 1 tablespoon lemon juice
- 2 tablespoons raw honey
- ¼ cup chopped avocado

Directions:

- Wash and rinse the kidney beans then place in a container with a lid.
- Pour water to cover the beans then covers the container with the lid and soaks the

beans overnight—3 cups water for 1-cup beans.
- In the morning, rinse and strain the beans.
- Pour water into a pot then bring to boil.
- Once it is boiled, stir in the kidney beans then cook for an hour.
- Strain the cooked kidney beans then place in a salad bowl.
- Drizzle raw honey and lemon juice over the beans then mix until the beans are completely coated with honey and lemon.
- Add chopped avocado into the bowl then mix well.
- Transfer to a serving dish then enjoy!

Lentils Balls Tomato Soup

Serving: 4

Nutrition Facts
Servings: 4
Per Serving
Calories 245
Total Fat 4.5g
Saturated Fat 0.7g
Trans Fat 0g
Cholesterol 0mg
Sodium 75mg
Potassium 613mg
Total Carb 37g
Dietary Fiber 15.7g
Sugars 3.1g
Protein 14.8g
Nutrition Facts
Servings: 4
Per Serving
Calories 245

30 DAY PULSES CHALLENGE

Ingredients:

1 cup cooked lentils

3 cups water

2 teaspoons minced garlic

¼ cup breadcrumbs

1 organic egg white

¼ cup chopped onion

1-tablespoon olive oil

¼ teaspoon pepper

¼ teaspoon nutmeg

¼ cup chopped tomato

2 tablespoons tomato paste

Directions:

- Place lentils in a pot then pour water over the lentils. Bring to boil.
- Once it is boil, covers the pot with the lid then reduces the heat.
- Cook for about 30 minutes until the lentils are tender.
- Place lentils in a food processor together with minced garlic, breadcrumbs, and egg white.
- Process until smooth then shape into medium balls.
- Preheat a pan over medium heat then pours olive oil into it.
- Once it is hot, place the balls on the pan then fry until brown.

30 DAY PULSES CHALLENGE

- Flip the balls and continue frying until both sides are brown.
- Strain from the oil then place on a plate.
- Preheat a saucepan over medium heat then pour the remaining olive oil into the saucepan.
- Once it is hot, stir in chopped onion then sautés until wilted and aromatic.
- Pour the liquid from the lentils into the saucepan then add chopped tomato and tomato paste into the pan.
- Season with pepper and nutmeg then bring to boil.
- Once it is boiled, add the lentils balls into the saucepan and bring to a simmer.
- Transfer to a serving dish then enjoy!